AUSTRALIA THE RACIAL CASTE SYSTEM

Copyright © 2024 Sushil Suresh

All rights reserved

Published by Sushil Suresh

First Edition: December 2024

ISBN eBook: 978-1-7638253-0-7

ISBN Paperback: 978-1-7638253-1-4

Thank you for buying an authorised edition of this book and for complying with copyright laws by not reproducing, scanning, or distributing any part of it in any form without permission.

Design: Bjorn Xavier

Contents

Racial Caste and Australia 1

Race and the Workforce 27

The White Norm 53

Immigration and race neutrality. 71

Racial caste and opportunity hoarding. 95

Diversity and the Politics of Data 105

Temporary Migration and the White saviours. 121

The Nostalgia for the White Home 151

The Latté Line. 169

Immigration and Segregation 193

1
Racial Caste and Australia

Discrimination dominates discussion about racism in Australia, although race/racism is more than just a matter of discrimination. In fact, it is well known that anti-discrimination, diversity, equal opportunity and so on are ways of dealing with a larger social problem at the level of individual behaviour, and/or organisational culture that discourage consideration of the wider societal framework. If racism is a matter of individual aberration, then the social organisation of Australian life, towards a logic and pattern of stratification based on race, and the consequences this has for everyday life, are not up for consideration. Further, individual behaviour is excised from the social processes that inform and necessitate customs, conventions, and personality traits. We have come to think of race and racism as two different matters; individuals can be members of, and hence socialised by, a race, and act as though their "individual" interests were not the promotion of the hegemony of one race against others. Individual actions are required to conform to the needs of a social terrain that values character, ability, and similar attributes over race or cultural background. Whether character, personality, actions, and abilities can be race-neutral is never questioned, although in everyday life we attribute all of these, in different and often contradictory ways, to an individual's race. In a globalised world, the shadow of White Australia seems to be receding, especially in "hyper-diverse" urban settings like Sydney. Many have even pronounced the "death of White Australia".

The story is that government fiat ended the era of White Australia, ushering in a new era of immigration and multiculturalism. The ideas of change and progress that inform this narrative set the terms of the debate on race and society, and shape the discourses on contemporary Australia and its ideas of racial intercourse and harmony. According to this worldview, despite limitations, the current state of race relations has moved on from its troublesome past, and is by far among the best in the world. In the public sphere, and in everyday social life, the idea that Australian society does not mirror race relations prevailing in the rest of the White West is prevalent. "Australian egalitarianism" ensures social relations characterised by relative racial harmony. This nationalistic creed of colour-blindness stems from another widely held belief in Australia's unique culture resulting from its perceived distance culturally, and geographically, from the troubled histories of race relations in the Americas or South Africa.

These ideas of progress based on pluralism and democracy set the agenda for Australia's future political destiny, when racism will have given way to a multi-racial or post-racial future society. Such social imaginaires also arise from and give expression to the belief that Australia is unlike other parts of the world that struggle to move beyond old traditions. Australia is seen as free of the religious, racial, and ethnic strife that have characterised the recent histories of much of the rest of the world. The implications of this belief in the newness of Australia are widespread: their formative presence can be traced from the grand social debates of the public sphere to the most inconspicuous customs and practices of everyday life. So deeply ingrained and impervious to challenge is this belief in the difference of Australia compared to non-western societies that everyday practices resembling social behaviours in the non-west are not considered similarities but rather fundamental human traits of kinship, human nature, or human failings.

The Australian ethos then would seem to be a type of ethnocentrism, preceding all politics, an innocent ur culture not tainted by the constitution of political projects and social hierarchies. In other words, the politics and culture of Australia are seen as fundamentally different to the politics of caste, communalism, religion, sect, or tribalism that characterise social life in Asia or Africa.

Accordingly, the current moment in Australian history is the outcome, from within its internal "White Western" history, and not marked by racial oppression, of a progressive development in its recent past enabling several races and cultures to co-exist and work together. We have here a picture that, tied to the self-image of a society, creates an ethos, a social order that taps into and strives to build on a tendency towards togetherness. Australia is not America, or South Africa—it has steered clear of racial antagonism; and it is not China, India, or Indonesia, held back by tradition, corruption, and poverty. The power of this nationalistic idea over the imagination and its ability to gloss over the nature of the local as a benign manifestation of a larger global racial order is immense. This Australian ideology builds on the fact of distinctness arising from distance and separateness, and the variations these enable in the local. That Australia's history and the big events in its history—for instance its recent history of mass immigration—resonate with the politics of race relations in the Americas, for example, have no room in these beguiling pictures of contemporary social reality. What matters then is the perceived distance from the current and past histories of Europe and America, and Asia and Africa.

Accordingly, this distance has created a local political community and a social order shorn of the worst excesses of racial imperialism, and settler colonialism. Where these exist, they are lingering traces of a troubled but dead past, and are in a relatively attenuated form—social problems that can be resolved within the Australian ambit. The Australian political system has inbuilt mechanisms to self-correct, and is capable of accommodating democratic changes. The socio-historical fact that the apparatus of representative government and its administrative machinery were forged through racial imperialism counts for little. The perceived spatio-temporal distance of Australia to the social programs of slavery and apartheid means that Australian society, its ethos, political institutions, culture, folklore, customs, mores, and conventions are not fundamentally racialised and/or organised for racial hegemony. This perceived distance is also ground for the denial of widely-prevalent local varieties of racial slavery and segregation that characterised Australia's history. It is almost as if racial slavery has an essence that the organisation of work and life in Australia deviated from.

The institutions that guide public and private life in Australia are believed to be race neutral. The preponderance of White Australians in these institutions is natural given Australia's White ethnic majority. Whether these institutions, designed to promote the rule of ethnic/racial majoritarianism through the party system and elections, through a system of trades and professions, can accommodate or reflect diversity is a matter seldom discussed in Australia. The doxa is that these institutions are amenable to diversity in terms of the personnel who can gain entry. Diversity is touted as the antidote to inequality and disparity in social life. The institutions of politics, i.e., the institutions of Australian public life, are race-neutral, and capable of realising democratic diversity and racial equality and harmony. Change in the form of a specific diversity, i.e., diversity in the workforce, in politics, or in the suburbs, is seen as progress, and evidence of the fundamentally egalitarian nature of Australia.

Such a distinct polity, a distinct society, necessitates the situating of local problems in this imaginary locale remote from South Africa or Brazil.

Since the local is encountered and managed through the national and its apparatus of governance, there are valid practical reasons for keeping a problem within the local context of its manifestation. But such practical necessities, in minimising the workings of a global order of racial hierarchy, serve to promote the colour-blind ideology of cultural pluralism and the race relations it enables. All of these are situated within the imaginary national. Such a cultural understanding of the Australian, which emphasises a culture free of politics or ethnicity, is an example of the national/local stripped of all that determined its past, and the ongoing political necessities that are a continuation of this past in a changing world.

There is then the common way of resorting to the "economy" and the "economic" to understand the "local" as it takes shape in relation to the "global". The immediacy of this pressing "economic" "fact" creates a compelling consensus among learned and ordinary everyday people. The problems of Australian communities are the everyday problems of social life, regardless of time and place. The changes in Australia then are the outcomes of changes in the global economy and the labour market. The choice of the economy/economics then serves to neutralise the importance of race. Since the economy is overarching—the human scramble for goods and commodities, the basic necessities of life—race/racism becomes a matter of discrimination. Lessening economic inequality means better or equal access to resources that are the neutral necessities for life; this then will lead to better race relations. These are examples, two sites, culture and economy, where the particularities of the Australian locale are commonly staged in ways that de-emphasise the racial nature of the local.

While it is important to localise the study of "local" social phenomena, it is impossible to evaluate anything "local" in a framework that is not comparative. In other words, there is no engagement with the social that is not always already comparative.

And comparison is guided by the choices and decisions regarding the emphases. Such emphases, and the peculiar neutrality that the terrain of the economy or culture permit, are all part of the lore that make up the idea of an Australia that is different. Making comparisons in the interpretation of the social, not just by expert observers but also everyday people, is a way of, through selective emphases, minimising the global and valorising the local in its economic or cultural particularity.

To restate, the choices made in speaking of or writing about or researching Australian social phenomena are the choices determined by socio-cultural/political proclivities, in this instance the belief that the current moment in Australia is a radical departure from its colonial past, and is a time of mass migration and multiculturalism working towards an inclusive social fabric. The tendency to study social problems within a certain framework, for instance the nationalistic methodologies of the social sciences, or the journalistic choice of speaking of race as a matter of discrimination or political correctness, are ways of looking away from the racial logics of current phenomena in an attempt not to talk about a fundamental social issue. While it would be easy to see this silence as a type of complicity it is also a way of not speaking about what cannot be changed, and instead focusing on what the possibilities are within the current state of affairs. The usual practice of resorting to the "economy" while discussing society, inequality, or exploitation is also often a ritualised manner of debate/discussion that steers ideas of society into a circumscribed realm of pluralism, inclusion, equality, change, and justice that then keep race out of the equation or reduce it to the status of an epiphenomenon. These strategies of avoidance and ways of talking about racism in Australia arise from a state of affairs integral to the maintenance of race relations as they are. Diversity, discrimination, multicultural affairs, funding for ethnic bodies and similar programs and slogans are all features of contemporary society that derive from an exclusionary social order rather than being signs of a pluralising socio-political situation.

Discussions that hymn the virtues of multiculturalism, ethnic diversity, and immigration are all so many varieties of nationalisms mystifying the caste order that is contemporary Australia. These are the furthest reaches of the progressive in Australia. Yet the social and political terrain these discourses on diversity legitimate do little to permit the racial nature of society to come to the fore.

When the history of Australia is seen as the history of a White nation that recently opened its doors to mass immigration and multiculturalism, the tendency to periodise history creates the impression of radical change. Such a belief in change also creates the agenda to look at society with new eyes, in order to understand phenomena that seem new. This is not just something that happens in everyday life, but is a characteristic feature of other types of social knowledge that claim the status of science, or theory. It is hard to miss the striking parallels between everyday conversations and social scientific or journalistic understandings of Australia. Both of these maintain a steadfast loyalty to the nationalistic creed of a plural Australia. As an example, the problems of a migrant are commonly seen as the problems of an outsider or a recent entrant. The problems of religious minorities are seen as the problems of cultural particularities. Racism is seen as a factor among other socio-economic factors. The fact that race always already structures the social field, even as it interacts with what is considered class or culture, is given little consideration. Racism/race then is a field of action called Australia that informs and determines nearly the entire gamut of human behaviour.

The nationalistic discourses on society, change, and continuity work towards minimising the role of race in everyday life, especially on matters of inequality. The specific manner of talking about inequality as "economic", and marginalisation as socio-cultural—arising from the circumstances of residency, migration, language, religion—are ways of denying/minimising the workings of race/racialisation in Australia. So, contemporary diversity resulting from mass migration is a new phenomenon that needs to be viewed in its specificity, keeping at bay the old Australia. This diversity then is also often relied upon to change the old. More often than not, White Australia is seen or considered as perfectly at ease with the diversity that surrounds it; as one among the many cultures that make up the fabric of local multiculturalism. It is almost as if White Australia has blended in with the rest of Australia, and in that process disappeared from the current historical moment, except as the remnant of a past era. However, White Australia is also synonymous with Australia and is taken to be a socio-cultural entity, analysed as Western society, distinct from the more recent arrivals—a neutral local norm.

The fabric of contemporary social life then is an elaborate web spun from hope, belief, myth, propaganda, fact, interpretation, and dogma that structures social fields and action. It would seem, given the prevailing ideologies/dogmas, that there are ways of acting in Australia that are purely human ways of acting, that one's actions are not pre-determined or over-determined; that opportunity and justice are open and democratic; that, given the fact of general affluence, upward mobility is race neutral; that multiculturalism means wealth and its symbols are neutral, and can be acquired across cultural or social boundaries; that poverty or marginalisation are "economic" phenomena and not the outcome of racial stratification/segregation. It is almost as if economic factors operate in a vacuum, except when it is the culture of the immigrant that can be an impediment to economic betterment.

When what is called the host society and its culture are seen as normative, the functioning of this norm in the economic, i.e., how the norm interacts and structures the economic, is not a problem at all. It is seldom acknowledged that the ethno-racial norm/the White norm structures the economic, the social, the cultural towards its political necessities for hegemony. The common practice of discussing contemporary society as a departure from past forms of social life due to transformations in the economy and work has created unquestioning assumptions and generalisations in relation to the economy or labour or society or history. In the case of contemporary Australia, these assumptions and generalisations about its economy and society are revealing and instructive. To anticipate the argument that follows, Australia's economic success is attributed to industrialisation and other social and economic phenomena synonymous with modern history. In social scientific knowledge and contemporary folkore, the transformations industrialisation subjects nations and societies to are usually subject to processes of selective interpretation and emphases that hide the way in which older forms of kinship, community, and social boundaries proliferate in renewed forms. While old relationships may not endure in recongnisable forms through historical time, their survival is ensured through a constant process of reinvention and reconstitution. The race relations of Australia should then be viewed as a historical process of constant renegotiation and reconstitution, enabling the old patterns of hegemony to endure in time through a process that envelops the entire socio-cultural terrain of society.

Multiculturalism took shape through mass migration. A few decades ago, Australia opened its doors to non-White immigration due to the need to populate the country and to deal with shortages in the labour force. While the timing may have varied in the other English speaking countries, mass immigration from the Global South to countries like Australia and Canada took off a few years apart. This convergence in immigration to these nations is seen as the result of transformations in the global economy and politics—the rich countries of the north were prosperous; they needed more labour for their growing economies. The story of immigration is usually narrated as a story of economic processes, and migration is viewed as a social process with dynamics of its own. Race is a problem that keeps rearing its ugly head in this narrative of economics and transnational social processes. People move from less developed regions of the world to affluent parts for better opportunities and a better life. Again, the norm of a better life is often portrayed as just economic, not cultural or symbolic. Of course, there is no shortage of discussion on the class character of the social, or even of the ethno-cultural or racial aspect of it. Rarely do these critiques point to the requirements of a politics of racial hegemony shadowing the project of multiculturalism and mass immigration. It is as though change worked its way in a uniform manner, corroding and limiting the sphere of past cultures, ushering in a new arena of social realities. Pluralism leaves little room for viewing cultures/social forms as competitive in a terrain that has been shaped by racial imperialism.

Race and the production of urban space

In the production of the space called Australia, race was a key element in the conquest of the territory by and for a race of people, i.e., a people considering itself as a race. This race/collectivity subjugates the Indigenous people. The control of this territory is seen as the control of a landmass, by a race. However, in the conquest of this territory, the land was transformed through the work done on it by the conquering people. We then have a clearing of the land for a new state of affairs. A set of ready-made institutions imported but also adapted to local conditions to protect the new social form and its work, in all its variety, done on this land. This social construction of White Australian life is what historians like Warwick Anderson, Marilyn Lake, and Henry Reynolds have referred to as the "whitening" of Australia, the "religion of whiteness", and so on. This whitening of Australia is not just the whitening of the geographical or physical landscape, but equally of the social forms and the work that these forms necessitate. Seen this way, the landscape is inextricably intertwined with all the economic activity that builds up a White society, i.e., it is an ethno-racial formation. The historical evolution of this society and the norms enshrined in its economic activity are profoundly racial. It is not just the commonsensical notions of racialism, based on phenotype, cultural traits, folklore, memories, and so on that develop in a social unit based on ethnic/racial homogeneity after they were implanted in a new locale; it is the manner in which these self-understandings of the people are invested in the work they do to build a homeland for the race, in a time of nations, nationalism, and racial imperialism. The organisation of life and work in Australia then has a history — shrouded in innumerable local customs and conventions that tie work and life together—a raced history, a memory that cannot be separated from the so-called cultural life of a people.

It would be naïve to see an Australian home as just a dwelling place, a residence devoid of any other socio-cultural and historical memories. What makes these memories precious or sacrosanct, almost inviolable, is the communal socio-cultural effort that goes into making the Australian home, or workshop, or business, or office. In other words, the Australian way of life, and its racialised socio-economic and cultural assets are fundamental to the self-understanding and survival of this socio-racial unit. It may be objected that none of this is new: it is well known that the division of labour was racial in Australia; that social relations between White Australians and the rest were always determined by racial divides and hierarchies. It may also be objected that the same applies to the work of any human collectivity that identifies itself as a people. The point here is simply that our ideas of race/racism separate out these things that are not separable, except by force or wilfully ignoring the "sacred" dimensions of the Australian socio-racial that White Australia sees as its culture, its folklore—i.e., the economic work/assets, including the customs and conventions that came to thrive around these assets, hymning them as a work ethic, and a way of life.

An understanding of the sacred as a realm circumscribed by the religious and apart from the secular is an impoverished understanding of the sacred in relation to the racial socio-cultural history of Australia. Again, this social-racial form White Australia cannot be seen only as a historico-political unit, a nation, a race; the fabric of this unit was made up of all the work, the trades, the professions, the arts, the social knowledges, the customs, conventions, manners, the social fears and political anxieties that shaped these mores—these are all in complex ways synonymous with race, and a raced idea of society, culture, nation, and so on.

We have, then, not a people who were industrialised or modernised; what we have is rather a people who invested industrialisation, the modern economy, work, and society with a racialised social organisation and life. Such a historical distinction as industrialised society cannot and must not be viewed as a neutral/neutralising social process so far as traditional ascriptions are concerned. It may be said that this is all well known in the sociological literature, that industrialisation and mass society reinforce identities even as they work towards making their old forms unviable in modern society. What is important to bear in mind is that the institutions of contemporary society, like education, the professions, skills, or work are all commonly understood and studied as social phenomena that are not necessarily related to race; education, qualifications, professions, and work are seen as matters that transcend or can transcend race and other traditional identities, and lead to societies that work towards the common welfare of all the races/ethnicities in a nation. However, there is no reason, looking at recent history, the evolution of work, and the racialised division of labour in society, to think that work and the labour market are sites that promote integration or harmony. On the contrary, work and the labour market are central to, and precisely those sites where the racial hierarchy is reproduced and reinforced. It is also important not to restrict ideas of work to the way work is conventionally categorised and defined in the social sciences. This is to say that work is not paid employment, a job, a profession; it is all the work a community does towards the reproduction of its way of life, in this instance a way of life that has come through and endures through changes, a way of life organised towards socio-racial hegemony.

One of the central tenets of modern society is that education and the professions are pathways to upward mobility. Yet, Australia's educational system and the system of work and the professions are striking examples of how education and the professions reproduce the racial caste system in a manner that bears a striking resemblance, despite local variation, with

South Africa, Brazil, the USA. There are many reasons to think, considering these societies and the types of racial stratification happening through their economies, that what we are witnessing at the moment is a continuation of the imperial project of racial hegemony orchestrated through what Etienne Balibar calls the nation form, this time in the name of diversity and democracy.

A great deal is said about globalisation as an economic process that favours elite sections of society, particularly the upper classes and upwardly mobile people, and how it disfavours the poor in the Global South. Globalisation has created national and international opportunities for hegemonic classes in all parts of the world, the social sciences tell us. Further, it has led to the disintegration of older forms of work through the internet and digitisation. In the case of Australia, what needs to be kept in mind is the manner in which ethno-racial hegemony is maintained in this historical moment of unprecedented economic integration. Australia's trade relations with its neighbouring regions, and the nature of immigration into the country, are clear examples of historically-prevailing race relations exploiting new social and economic phenomena towards the maintenance of a traditional racial hierarchy. It could be said that the economy in Australia is subject to the need—this includes the digital economy and all new forms of work—of traditional racial symbols of status. These traditional hierarchies subject new forms of work towards reinforcing the White racial norm. This happens in domains of society, like the professions and education, that are built around cultural neutrality.

Writing on the White Australia policy, Andrew Markus says:

"After 1901, the freedom of non-European residents contracted steadily; communities atrophied as their members emigrated or died. Within white Australian society there was a growing racial arrogance, a ready acceptance of widening discriminatory practices, and an intolerance of diversity. The understanding of the concept of white races was refined as measures were adopted to restrict European immigration. These developments, particularly in the inter-war period, were in keeping with the growth of a bureaucratic state, with its concomitant striving for centralisation of power and consistency of practice, and are most evident in the control over Aboriginal populations. The White Australia policy played a role in nourishing, and was in turn nourished by the major currents in Australian life."

This state building and the centralisation that it required was the work of the Australian community. It created not just a communal ethos based on race and a belief in culture as a raced phenomenon but, as Markus explains, it not just justified racist behaviour, it also necessitated it. Importantly, this was not just a political act oriented towards state-building, it was also the communal, racial nation form that required a socio-racial political community and the modes of life this necessitated. We cannot view the details of everyday life or the personal habits of Australians as apolitical or innocent of the political requirements of racial hegemony. On the contrary, the entirety of personal life, the whole gamut of social existence, and the public domain of Australian life, i.e., the family, work, the arts, politics were all suffused with ideas of racial distinctness and caste privilege. This caste system necessitated the organisation of the economy and the polity, and the continuing subjugation of social life, to the needs of the racial hierarchy. It is naïve to think that a socio-historical program such as this, organised on a global scale, would wither away in a few generations.

The nature of work in Australia has always been determined by the racial hierarchy, be it in the time of its history as a colony, the rise of pastoralism, the gold rushes, agriculture, mass immigration, or multiculturalism. Faced with chronic labour shortages, Australia imports, and has always imported, labour into the country. The historic pattern of this labour migration into Australia has been shaped by the needs of racial imperialism and racial hegemony. The specific nature of the worker brought into Australia was always to fit into the needs of a racialised economy and culture of work designed to reproduce the racial caste system. This has been traditionally explained through the paradigms of discrimination, inhuman treatment of Indians, Afghans, Melanesians, coolies, the Chinese, etc

It is instructive here to quote from Lake and Reynolds:

"...the transnational circulation of emotions and ideas, people and publications, racial knowledge and technologies that animated white men's countries and their strategies of exclusion, deportation and segregation, in particular, the deployment of those state-based instruments of surveillance, the census, the passport and the literacy test. The project of whiteness was thus a paradoxical politics, at once transnational in its inspiration and identifications but nationalist in its methods and goals. The imagined community of white men was transnational in its inspiration and identifications but nationalist in its outcomes, bolstering regimes of border protection and national sovereignty."

[...]

"In drawing the colour line, immigration restriction became a version of racial segregation on an international scale, as Lothrop Stoddard

memorably stated. Not surprisingly, the education or literacy test, first used to disenfranchise black voters in Mississippi in 1890, also became the basis of United States immigration restriction laws, promoted by Anglo-Saxonists such as Henry Cabot Lodge and the members of the Boston-based Immigration Restriction League, legislation which served in turn as a model for Natal and the other British Dominions. The republican origins of the literacy test as an instrument of racial exclusion were significant. In dividing the world into white and not-white it helped render the imperial non-racial status of British subjects increasingly irrelevant and provided a direct challenge to the imperial assertion that the Empire recognized no distinction on the basis of colour or race...

"Histories of immigration policy, like studies of whiteness, have usually been told as self-contained national stories, their dynamics located in distinctive local reactions against particular groups of foreign immigrants — whether Chinese, Indian, Islanders, Japanese, Jews or southern Europeans. Some historical studies have, to be sure, identified parallel developments in Australasia, British Columbia and New Zealand and on the west coast of the United States. Usually, however, their stories have remained parallel, rather than dynamically inter-connected and thus mutually formative. What most histories have tended to miss is what DuBois could see clearly, that is, the significance of racial identifications to the constitution of modern political subjectivities and ways of being in the world, in a process that shaped white men's sense of collective belonging to a larger community..."

As mentioned earlier, ideas of discrimination are more in the nature of a plea, through debunking myths on harmonious race relations, for fair and humane treatment in a social system based on race. These pleas are calls for reform, ongoing attempts to humanise relations that arise from historical ideas of domination and servitude. This is to say that the nature of immigration into Australia in the 19th and 20th century was over-determined in all its aspects by the needs of racial hegemony.

One can chart the evolution of migration into Australia as a history of the progressive acceptance of "equality" in labour and in social life of the non-European; or one can see this history as a continual adaptation or survival of racial hegemony in changing circumstances. Historians of race relations in Australia have documented the violence and brutality that was characteristic of work in all Australian industries that employed non-White labour. This violence was built into the specific methods of recruiting and managing non-European labour in all forms of work, from the use of Indigenous labour to practices like blackbirding, in Australian industries faced with shortages. These shortages are often explained in a conventional economic way, i.e., that White workers were unavailable for certain types of work where the wages were low. This is a technique of stripping the economic of its racial aspects that are inextricably tied to the cultural mores and lifestyles of a caste. This is to say that certain forms of work are incompatible with maintaining one's caste status, and so are unviable for members of a dominant group. It is important to keep in mind that the numbers of workers/immigrants were as crucial as the nature of the work they were expected to do, in the 19th century and into the 21st century. Markus says in *Australian Race Relations* that although the number of non-Europeans who worked under Europeans was only a small part of the population, the manner in which they were used was crucial not just for industry in Australia but equally for the system of race relations that were becoming the social norm. Markus says that the system of occupational discrimination prevented Melanesians and other non-Europeans, like the Chinese or Japanese, from engaging in occupations that were reserved for European labour. The restriction of immigration into Australia and the organisation of work were all part of the plan to build a society and way of life based on racial distinctions.

The conditions of employment of non-Europeans were crucial not just for the profitability of industries like commercial farming but also for the status distinctions that were important for the caste system based on White and non-White. Among the reasons adduced were biological ideas of race that reflected widely-held beliefs that White labour was not suited to working in certain climates and that non-White work was more suited to certain conditions of work. We have here an example of a racial system of caste influencing ideas of work and a social organisation of life that necessitates an economy based on racialised forms of work. Further, importantly, we need to bear in mind the similarities this Australian pattern of social life has—despite the variations that are adaptations to local circumstances including geography, demography, the global political conditions for the availability of labour, and the cultural norms informing racialised patterns of work—with other settler colonial societies. Australian writers have usually emphasised the differences to refute the existence of slavery and segregation, as if these cultural forms have to resemble a supposedly-prototypical model developed in South Africa or the United States. What we have, then, is a socio-political system based on racial hegemony developed and maintained in different parts of the world to suit varied conditions but working towards a political program of ethno-racial privilege.

In their introduction to *Drawing the Global Colour Line*, Marilyn Lake and Henry Reynolds, discussing the writings of W B DuBois on global race relations, write:

"By 1910, it was also clear to DuBois that the problem of the colour line was the problem of what he called 'whiteness', which had recently acquired the force of a charismatic religion: 'Wave upon wave, each with increasing virulence, is dashing this new religion of whiteness on the shores of our time.' DuBois saw in this tidal wave of whiteness a new, modern, phenomenon [...] Whiteness provided a mode of subjective identification that crossed national borders and shaped global politics. 'What is whiteness,' DuBois wondered, 'that one should so desire it?' Whiteness, he realised, was fundamentally proprietorial [...]"

Lake and Reynolds chart the *"spread of 'whiteness' as a transnational form of racial identification, that was, as DuBois noticed, at once global in its power and personal in its meaning, the basis of geo-political alliances and a subjective sense of self. The emergence of self-styled 'white men's countries' represented whiteness in defensive, but defiant, mode, a response to the rising power of what Charles Pearson, a Liberal politician in the colonial parliament of Victoria, had named, in* 'National Life and Character: A Forecast', 'the black and yellow races'".

It is by thinking of the new as a terrain on which the old keeps reinventing itself that we can trace the history of work and life in Australia. Looking at the new as a break from the past or as change only hides the enduring nature of the old forms of work and status, and the social life these arise from, in Australia. No doubt there are problems inherent in this type of questioning directed at social forms. Are we trying to say that the old has an essence? At what point in history does the old constitute itself as an autonomous social form that maintains a core or essence through changes in time? What conditions permit a particular set of social relations to emerge as a form that shapes changes in time that social relations are subjected to? Isn't racial privilege subject to change and modification to the point of erosion, like all other social phenomena? What time scale or periodisation can help locate and problematise change?

Since discussions of race relations are concerned with questions about the contemporary, we can only aim to describe social processes that seem to determine the spatio-temporal moment we live in. To repeat current ideas in the social sciences, we must keep in mind that social relations are not universal timeless essences; they are processes subject to the spatio-temporal exigencies that condition our perception. Race relations and our ideas of race are constantly changing as social configurations realign. It is worthwhile to bear in mind that questions about the nature of "change and continuity" as they relate to social phenomena are often pushed too far not just for epistemological reasons but also to promote an attitude of resignation to the status quo. There is a way of legitimising Australian race relations through a belief that it is in the natural order of things; that inequality and unequal access are global realities that manifest in more humane ways in Australia. It is also common to contrast contemporary diversity and immigration to the state of affairs prevailing in Australia a few decades ago, and hence conclude that we are in a phase that is a progressive outcome of developments in recent history. These attitudes are prevalent in everyday life as well as among observers who generate expert commentary/ analyses of Australia. It is as if the ethno-racial project is a natural given, a universal state, and social relations based on segregation, marginalisation, and inequality have to be analysed as problems that are not related to this socio-racial.

If we, however, decide to look at the current conjuncture as a social state flowing on from and shaped by what preceded it in Australia, it would be hard to deny the social facts of racial hegemony that structure contemporary life and work. Rather than looking at modern Australia as a changed entity, transformed by the global economy and labour market, we can also view Australia's labour market and workforce as phenomena structured by past patterns of race relations. Surely the global economy and changing labour market have transformed work, and created new modes of social existence, but the workings of racial hegemony mean that the politico-economic necessities of immigration and the distribution of occupations, work and income among the several races in Australia are further instances of ethno-racial stratification and the consolidation of a racial caste system. These phenomena, together with the patterns of urban segregation and education, constitute a racialised economy and society that reproduce traditional forms of prestige and status.

Works referred to

1. Tavan, Gwenda. 2005 . *The long, slow death of white Australia*, Scribe.
2. Markus, Andrew *Australian Race Relations: 1788-1993* (Australian Experience). 1994. Allen & Unwin.
3. Reynolds, Henry, Lake, Marilyn. 2008. Dr*awing the global colour line: White men's countries and the international challenge of racial equality*, Cambridge University Press.

2

Race and the Workforce

As mentioned earlier, in contemporary society we look at work through the prism of jobs, careers, and the individual; the employed and the unemployed and so on, all related to concepts like homo economicus, and individual agents. Many of the social dimensions of work are de-emphasised or completely obfuscated by these atomised, individualised frameworks that shape analyses and discussion of labour. The social aspect that these paradigms permit is a collectivity populated by individual job seekers and workers with skills and qualifications. So, for instance, we have the problematics of race/racism discussed only through discrimination. The ethno-racial nature of work, and how this manifests in skills and jobs, is rarely permitted any room in this picture painted with ideas of neutrality that inform theories about jobs, education, skills, and work. It would seem, going by these prevailing ideas, that nursing is just nursing, especially in a globalised world where nurses from the Global South migrate in droves for work to the richer parts of the world; similarly, we tend to think a driver's job is just that, to drive, whether it's in New York, Dubai, or Sydney; we think that the professions are guided by professional standards of certification and other industry-related norms of professionalism and work; and we think that teaching is mostly a matter of instructing/initiating students into a body of codified knowledge that has been crafted largely through scientific/culture-neutral terms. It is as though these skills and the forms of work that are done through them are not appropriated by a plethora of local ethno-cultural norms and mores that work towards very specific local socio-political means and ends. This is to say that the arena of work, and the culture and cultural lore that shroud any local labour market, are shot through with competitive politics and political agendas that are ethno-cultural in ways that are specific to local cultures. In this instance we need to keep in mind the socio-racial that governs all aspects of Australian life, from the deeply private and personal to the most public. We need to bear in mind the collective nature of the Australian socio-racial that structures work to not just reflect the personal or the familial or the community, but also to nurture, nourish, and protect these from corroding encroachments. This is the sacred aspect of the socio-racial that is White Australia, i.e., race as community and the communal, race as life itself, not just biologically but socio-culturally.

The problems related to the transference of skills from one culture to another are well known in Australia. Such problems then call for the initiation of, for example, nurses into the Australian health system and its cultural ways of caring. This period of training, when a worker transitions from Kenya to Sydney, is a time when, in the same trade across two nations, an immigrant learns how to fit into a new labour market. This labour market is also loaded with its local cultural norms, and a system of penalties and rewards. We then must think of a system of nursing that is a patchwork of local norms and global standards. It would be impossible to think of a universal style of nursing happening in an Australian health care facility. What would this universal style be? Would a Chinese or Iranian way of nursing, unvarnished by Australian work practices and culture, be acceptable to an Australian? If we consider other examples, for instance a Pakistani accountant working for an Australian entertainment business that needs to grow its business globally but remain headquartered in Australia: are the numbers just a matter of numbers, always? Let us consider a teacher of economics or philosophy trying to pursue a career in Australia: it becomes clear then that the limitations and professional impediments facing these workers are, as is well known, largely what is termed cultural. This cultural is the socioracial that regulates and determines the nature of work in Australia, as it has in the past with Aboriginal workers, Melanesians, Afghans, Chinese, or coolies.

In this era of colourblindness it is easily assumed that the modern workforce is a break from Australia's colonial past; today, Australia, as a modern economy, is in need of skills in many sectors of its globalising economy. These skills shortages plague several sectors of the economy, from medicine and engineering to retail and factory work.

The current immigration program would seem to be designed to fill these shortages by giving preference to skilled migration over all other categories of migrants. The processes to determine these skills shortages in the local labour market are a matter of endless debate and controversy. Several interests—including professional associations, unions, and businesses that need more labour and skills available locally—put forward competing views, based on their research models, advocating different migration regimes. This debate on migration is instructive: the issues are Australia's need for a larger population, which means more workers and consumers fuelling economic growth; the need to service an ageing population; then the need for workers for the major infrastructure upgrades that are urgent in Australia; again the needs of a diverse multicultural workforce that will make Australia look like a contemporary migrant nation capable of engaging with global society; and, last but not least, the need to ensure there are enough people in the workforce to support an ageing population. All these demographic and economic issues have to be balanced against the race issue, which today, of course, is spoken of in the language of colour blindness.

We know that Australia's migration program is biased in favour of skilled migrants. These migrants are younger, educated, and in broad terms categorised as skilled migrants and/or professionals. Skilled migrants are also known to be in the workforce at a rate that is higher than the rate of participation for locals. Local research confirms the "fact" that many migrants work as "professionals" after settlement in Australia, even if they are not able to find opportunities in the professions they pursued in their home countries. This is to say they work in a job categorised as "professional" or "associate professional". Yet when we look around the big cities of Australia, non-Europeans dominate certain industries and trades—the hyper visibility of non-Europeans in the low wage, low statused sectors of the economy is a consequence not just of their numerical preponderance in these sectors but also because White Australians are averse to these sectors dominated by immigrants. In scholarly circles, the common reasons given for this phenomenon are economic, the circumstances related to finding suitable employment in a new country; and the social reason is that natives look for more prestigious work. In everyday life though, it is common to hear these low wage sectors referred to as immigrant jobs. It is important to keep in mind that the circumstances forcing immigrants from the Global South to work in factories or as cleaners, security guards, or drivers do not apply to immigrants from the UK, US, or Europe. We need to look at this structure of the labour market as a striking feature of the racial caste system and its manner of stratification, i.e., the distribution of White and White-like workers in prestigious or stable or lucrative/salaried occupations, and the concentration of non-European races in other sectors of the economy.

In this context we must try to see the historically racialised nature of work and the workforce in Australia, from its earliest days as a colony, and the successive phases of its racial economy—its use of Aboriginal labour in particular occupations, its importation of non-Europeans for certain types of work, its recruitment practices and its treatment of these workers, the proscriptions on the types of employment for non-European workers—as the historico-political foundation for an ongoing pattern of labour force management and the organisation of work and life towards traditional modes of racial status and privilege. As a social phenomenon, the over-representation of immigrants from the Global South in specific sectors of the labour market is a structural feature of all English-speaking and other labour-importing rich societies.

It should not be thought that there is no diversity in the Australian professions. What we see, however, and what the data don't tell us, given their methodological nationalism, is that the overall distribution of migrants from the Global South in certain sectors, as well as the manner of their distribution, i.e., the agenda of diversity, in occupations where they are not numerically dominant, are in keeping with the logics of Australia's racial caste system. About one-quarter of Australia's 14 million-strong workforce is made up of persons born overseas. It is believed that the prospects of these immigrants are determined by their visa status, the category under which they arrive in Australia, their education, English language ability, age, and so on.

Among the challenges of settlement for new migrants are the difficulties in finding suitable jobs that use their education, skills, and training. Discrimination is often cited as one of the reasons why new migrants struggle to get a foot in the workforce; it is also known that education and skills from the Global South are not always tailor-made for Australian conditions. There are concerns, then, about immigrants making exaggerated claims about their abilities and the quality of their education. Lack of local experience too is usually considered a reason for the inability of skilled migrants to break into the occupations they were in prior to arrival into Australia. It is said that many don't find employment in the first six months, in some cases even a year, after arrival. More than half of those immigrants categorised as "professional" experience downward mobility after arrival in Australia. The post-migration status of many immigrants is known to change from professional to labourer, once in Australia. However, importantly for both skilled and unskilled, employment in a rich nation is considerably more lucrative, and in the long run improves the average immigrant's financial situation. However, occupationally speaking, research has also revealed considerable downward mobility among skilled migrants from the Global South after their arrival into Australia. Such downward mobility is not associated with immigrants from the Global North; what is not discussed or anaylsed in the literature is how race or ethnocultural attributes determine labour force outcomes among migrants. That said, a combination of factors determines the prospects of workers from the third world in Australia. Among these are the demand and supply factors: for instance, the largest group of permanent arrivals in Australia, selected on the basis of skills, education, age, and English language ability, is from India (at the time of writing in 2021). Together with other nationalities from the South Asian region, this group is the largest group of professional and/or educated migrant jobseekers in Australia; this group from India is followed by China, the UK, the Philippines, and Malaysia. The labour force outcomes of all these groups from the Global South lag significantly behind the labour force outcomes of immigrants from the UK. Lack of networks, English language difficulties, and credential disparities are among the reasons cited for this outcome, apart from the fact that immigrant groups from the third world usually come from occupations that are oversupplied in Australia. This oversupply factor does not seem to affect the labour force outcomes of domestic Australian graduates in the labour market; there is no evidence that the situation of oversupply in certain occupations like accounting, engineering, or business management affects immigrants from the UK or Europe.

This situation has been described by some migration scholars as arising from an "ethnic penalty", a euphemism for racism and the high value placed on ethno-racial characteristics in the labour market. Further, the poor labour market outcomes of international students from the Global South with Australian qualifications—well over half of them are unable to find jobs in their field of education—is another trend showing that local education and networks are all racialised and work towards keeping the labour force segmented.

This problem of the fate of skilled migrants in Australia, the largest component of Australia's immigration program, is a matter that has aroused the concerns of scholarly observers and local governments. It is seen as a loss of valuable skills to the local economy. Given the assumptions the scholarly community has about the superiority or difference of work in Australia compared to work in the third world, the troubles of immigrants are attributed to adjustment issues, lack of English language skills, lack of local experience, and networks. Again, the role of discrimination is acknowledged occasionally.

An example of this style of framing is something like this: In the paper "Skilled Migration and the Workforce: An Overview", John Saunders states:

"In a review of results from the Longitudinal Survey of Immigrants to Australia (LSIA), Shah and Burke (2005) describe the labour market experiences of migrants and highlight some of the difficulties migrants face in securing a job, particularly one which matches their qualifications and training. They note that, while about three-quarters of permanent migrants to Australia over a one-year period from September 1999 had a job in the 12 months prior to migration, only a little over half had found a job in Australia within six months of arrival, this proportion increasing to about 60% over a further 12 months. Analysis by occupational profiles before and after migration suggests there is also considerable downward movement in occupational status as a consequence of migration, with many higher-qualified migrants unable to find jobs that match their skills and resulting in their having to resort to lower-level jobs. For example, while 62% of pre-migration jobs were as managers and administrators, professionals or associate professionals, only 41% of post-migration jobs were in these categories. By contrast, only 2% of pre-migration jobs were as labourers, but the post-migration proportion was 15%. Interestingly, the comparative proportions for tradespersons stayed relatively constant at around 12%."

The problem with discrimination

Given the racialised nature of Australian society, it is important to think critically about immigration research, and its nationalist methodologies. In the current moment in Australia, multiculturalism is touted as the progressive future enabling distinct peoples to co-exist. This has become a nationalistic creed, and is often touted as the path to a multi-racial or post racial future: multiculturalism is the socio-cultural political system that will realise a more harmonious future for Australia. This creed has become a methodological dogma in the social sciences, and in other forms of writing about society. It should not be thought that these research methods are not useful—they are indispensable knowledges that enable understanding of important aspects of the socius. However, we need to problematise the question of race here. On arrival in Australia, are immigrants from the third world seen as professionals? Or as members of a nation/race? In White Australian society, what has been the status of these races traditionally? Can we think that the subordinate status of non-White races in Australia had nothing to do with work and the Australian way of life? A "professional" from the third world puts up his hand for an Australian job: is this situation just a matter of a skilled worker looking for work? Is this "professional" seen as a professional or does he also represent the racial nature of migration into Australia? Does that determine perceptions related to his/her skills and ability to work in the system of Australian professions? Aren't these work situations loaded with historical meanings and associations? In other words, is the labour market race neutral? If not, how does it use race? To what end is race, a worker or professional's race, used for in the labour market? Just as the non-European immigrant's nationality determines her/his suitability or place in a racialised labour market, couldn't we say that the European's place in the labour market, regardless of skills or qualifications, is determined by race?

It is known that, unlike past phases of Australia's migration history, today's migrants are more qualified/educated than the average Australian worker. It is, of course, debatable if these qualifications are readily adaptable to a different society. Still, can we think of the labour market as a site where race relations are neutralised for the sake of skills necessary to do work that is necessary? What is the work that is necessary in Australia? Is there a consensus on this? Or should we think that the Australian way of life—and the nature of work, the types of labour and work that happens through it—was a fundamentally racialised mode of social existence? Couldn't we say that race, i.e., the socio-racial, determines not just the pattern of distribution of races in the Australian workforce, but also crucially the social purpose of this work? To put it differently, if the same work was to be carried out with a very different distribution of ethnicities in the different sectors of the economy, would it still be the same work, or the same society? Would it be acceptable to White Australia?

One important point to bear in mind when speaking of the economy of Australia is its ageing affluent population that is accustomed to an affluent aristocratic way of life, especially in relation to the rest of the global village. This aristocratic way of life is an economy that has created its own needs of labour too, in other words an economy and a labour market around an aristocratic affluent way of life.

If we stop looking at racism as just discrimination, if we decide to look at it as the emergence of a social order that shaped human relations and a worldview with all its hierarchies, culture, status, taboos, and rituals as arising from this racial order, we'd then see Australian society as we know it and live it as always already racialised. It is impossible and counter-productive to look at society as a social state that can transcend race. This fundamentally racialised nature of society is what needs to be factored in as the socio-racial—this is to say that modern mass society in its modes of life, its manner of historically organising life and work, has always been directed towards racial hegemony. It would be a limitation to see the labour market or work as not shaped by and responding to the needs of this caste system, which is the manifestation of a global order in a local setting.

The economic then cannot be seen as a separate realm from race; racialisation is predatory on the economy for its larger needs of hegemony, not just in labour relations and hierarchies, but additionally, fundamentally, in the entire forms that work takes shape in social life. In saying this, the idea is not to argue that race has an essence or identifiable core. However, it is important to call attention to the fact that so far as Australia is concerned, changing work practices, new occupations, skills, new forms of culture, and technology are all subject to the politics of racial hegemony.

In their classic work Racial formation in the United States, Omi and Winant write: *"A racial project is simultaneously an interpretation, representation, or explanation of racial identities and meanings, and an effort to organize and distribute resources (economic, political, cultural) along particular racial lines."* So far as the argument here is concerned, it is crucial to bear in mind that there is no economy, no resource (material, or symbolic) that is not always already racialised.

It should be clear from the preceding arguments that

discrimination is an epiphenomenon of a larger problem, which is the organisation of society. Definitions like the one just cited do not get us beyond this idea of discrimination. Earlier it was mentioned that work cannot be seen as separate from culture, from personal life, from politics, from family life, and so much more that constitutes the horizon of a community's social life. This is to say that work is an integral element of the socio-political existence of a community; one cannot see paid work and jobs as the entirety of a community's effort in the realm of work. These are important economic activities that are bolstered by and supplement numerous other forms of work that are not economic in the usual sense economic is taken to be; but these forms of social life are inseparably enmeshed with all strictly economic work; they include family, charity, neighbourhood networks, professional associations that overlap with family connections, business ties and networks, the arts, and scholarly research, activism and so on. All these activities together make up the community's social existence that cannot be disentangled from the world of jobs. From this enmeshed situation arises the need to celebrate the life and work of the ethno-racial community.

Blackface and the Australian workforce

Much has been written about art forms and cultural practices, for instance blackface, that denigrated African Americans and racial Others in the United States. These racialised art forms are seen as apart from a racial collectivity's everyday life. From this it would seem that the need to ridicule and denigrate the racial Other is not the concern of everyday life. When such art forms are singled out for their racism, it is assumed that other cultural forms that make up a community's cultural cannon are race-neutral. It is well known that this is hardly the case. It would be impossible to find an Australian cultural form or artistic activity that does not hymn the socio-racial. Art works that do not mention other races, it is well-known, are engaged in imagining into existence harmonious ethno-racial communities free of the troubling aspects of race, society, and history. These works are abundant in the cultural landscape of Australia, and have played an indispensable role in conjuring into existence a White Australia seen through its internal White history, with race as something that exists on the periphery. That is, whiteness is seen as ethno-cultural, biological, occurring in nature, and so on. Australian history (including what is termed creative writing, like novels) that has kept race at bay is an important example of genres that conjure into existence mythical harmonious communities. It would seem that these social histories of Australia are not immersed in racial concerns; that work, culture, society has an ethno-cultural core that pre-existed settler colonialism. In contrast, cultural forms and practices that resort to stereotyping, ridiculing, and denigrating racial others in an explicit manner are viewed as outmoded or undesirable practices in contemporary society, although they may still be prevalent. When racial stereotypes occur in cinema, music, literature, or in any form in the public sphere (say in a politician's speech), the producers of these works are sometimes castigated for their cultural insensitivity. Much is said then about the need for cultural appropriateness and political correctness.

In these practices we once again see the workings of a thinking oriented towards seeing racism as just discrimination. What is explicitly denigratory is disapproved of, but the racialised nature of culture, social norms, and the racialised world of work are not questioned. These are seen as natural social facts of an ethno-racial collectivity.

When work is seen as an integral part of a social unit's political life, practices of distancing and excluding the Other through creating boundaries based on merit, efficiency, or culture are a larger social matrix that enables the racial hierarchy to remain unchallenged. The nature of work is tied inseparably to the symbols of status, achievement, recognition, and success. These symbols of status, success, ability are all profoundly racialised. In other words, these are all ethno-cultural phenomena. So, the nature of work and the symbols of achievement and rewards in Australia cannot be viewed apart from the nature of the workforce as we see it today.

The public sphere in Australia has little room for diversity, except in certain predictable and specific forms that go towards celebrating the racial norm. The path to recognition and success in almost any field of activity in Australia then is clearly reserved for the White racial norm, and this ethno-racial aspect of success and recognition are integral to the social processes of racial hegemony. It would be impossible to separate these from all forms of work, and art, and how these aggregate towards a White racial norm and racial ideas of ability and talent. The racialised nature and symbols of merit, achievement, recognition, rewards, achievement, and success tell us a great deal about the politics of the socio-racial and its workings in everyday life. Surely, ability and achievement can be seen as a subjective individual matter, but this is another example of a way of restricting the discussion of work, art, culture, sport, achievement, rewards, and effort to the realm of the atomised individual.

When one looks at work in all its forms in Australia, from manual labour to intellectual work, it becomes clear that all forms of prestigious work, the work where accomplishments are valued and celebrated in public life, work that sacralises cultural norms of work, cultural norms of art, and work that is believed to be meritorious in private and public life, as well as work that is regarded respectable or skilled, are all forms of work dominated by White Australians. It would seem that talent, interest, choice, education, and training lead to these roles as builder, lawyer, professor, doctor, or artist. The vast cultural and institutional support systems that go into creating roles reserved for individuals from the White caste to stage White hegemony through the trades, the professions, and the arts are barely spoken of in contemporary discourse. This is a curious situation that parallels the picture painted by European historians of the Indian caste system. Not just are these institutions dominated by White Australians, the ethos that governs their work, the ideas of society that have shaped and guided their existence derive from the needs of racial hegemony through maintaining the racial caste system of Australia. One then sees a social matrix of institutions supporting forms of life and work that set White against the rest in a social process of competition for prestige and hegemony. It would be impossible to separate the free-standing

White Australian home from the work of the legal profession, the legal norm, the medical norm, or the social-scientific concerns and style/s of the Australian academic or journalist; it would be impossible to separate the White norm and the White home from the work relations that take shape, as though set by nature in stone, on the factory floor or the construction site or a loading dock or restaurant kitchen. In all these forms of work, racial hegemony is paramount, and the actors, selected mostly based on phenotype (after a period of apprenticeship, if that is necessary), fill these roles with what is required in terms of the duties that go with a role that is a socio-political necessity for Australia's racial caste system. As mentioned earlier, it is, for instance, not the economy or economics that matters here, but it is the phenotype of the person who has mastered the workings of the economy that is crucial in public life.

Mastery and phenotype are inseparable; diversity in the workforce permits expertise to all races, but racial hegemony requires the Australian voice to be of only one phenotype. Again, it would be a mistake to see this mastery residing in the individual; rather it is the vast matrix of cultural and social networks and forces, the socio-racial, that naturalises the presence of this phenotype, as a logical outcome of numerical majority in the population, as arising from the historical life of a social unit, from personal aptitude, leanings and so on. The politics of this mastery—the image of this figure in the public sphere, as expert, as artist, as leader, as toiler, as rebel—towards ensuring the continuing hegemony of the racial norm in the workforce cannot be overestimated. This norm, then, is not a neutral norm; it is a qualification, an eligibility, a requirement, a suitability, the lack of which makes the racial other less desirable for certain sectors of the economy and realms of society. Work is then not just work; accounting or nursing or French philosophy are not what they are meant to be if not practised by or embodied in a White phenotype. Nor is it the case that any of these actors and the professions they practice are separable from the racialised modes of social life that lead to these occupations. Verbally, or at the level of ideas, it is easy to challenge and dismiss this as irrational; it is also often seen as resulting from a lack of clear understanding of the social realities, i.e., the demographics behind the "realities" of the workforce.

What is the White man?

In Racial formation in the United States, Omi and Winant say:
"Race is a concept that signifies and symbolizes social conflicts and interests by referring to different types of human bodies. Although the concept of race invokes seemingly biologically based human characteristics (so-called phenotypes), selection of these particular human features for purposes of racial signification is always and necessarily a social and historical process. Indeed, the categories employed to differentiate among human beings along racial lines reveal themselves, upon serious examination, to be at best imprecise, and at worst completely arbitrary ...

"Despite the problematic nature of racial categorization, it should be apparent that there is a crucial and non-reducible visual dimension to the definition and understanding of racial categories. Bodies are visually read and narrated in ways that draw upon an ensemble of symbolic meanings and

associations. Corporeal distinctions are common; they become essentialized. Perceived differences in skin color, physical build, hair texture, the structure of cheek bones, the shape of the nose, or the presence/absence of an epicanthic fold are understood as the manifestations of more profound differences that are situated within racially identified persons: differences in such qualities as intelligence, athletic ability, temperament, and sexuality, among other traits.

"Through a complex process of selection, human physical characteristics ("real" or imagined) become the basis to justify or reinforce social differentiation. Conscious or unconscious, deeply ingrained or reinvented, the making of race, the 'othering' of social groups by means of the invocation of physical distinctions, is a key component of modern societies. 'Making up people,' once again. This process of selection, of imparting social and symbolic meaning to perceived phenotypical differences, is the core, constitutive element of what we term 'racialization'."

We cannot and must not see phenotype as occurring in nature; we must not think that corporeal differences exist to be perceived, and categorised socially, because corporeal distinctions and presumed biological characteristics are co-constituted in the emergence of society, i.e., the socio-racial. In other words, a social state comes together, through work and ways of living, in all its variety and forms, and this social scenario is co-constituted with a phenotype that appears inseparable from this state of affairs. What we then have is a visual regime that produces not just race or the White phenotype, but all the cultural particularities, its social mores, and myths, the prohibitions that undergird its social existence in its entirety: this is to say the cultural ecosystem and habitat (its work, its customs and conventions, its ideals), so to speak, of the White race. Such a race exists and cannot stop existing so long as the cultural and political history that produced a distinct phenotype endures. In relation to contemporary society there is no race, no whiteness without the mise-en-scene, the socio-political and cultural ensemble that produces race. This is important to bear in mind while thinking of race as overarching, as much more than discrimination; we must keep this in mind while talking about race and work, the professions and upward mobility, equality and marginalisation, culture and the arts, politics and the economy, the White home and White careers and so on. The presence, the occurrence of phenotype in the socius is a production of all of these.

Race and the production of social spaces

What we call a place or a country is inseparable from the human ways of living, and the social collectives that live on that land. We tend to think of the land as a container, and the people as those who are the contents of that container. However, the spaces occupied by human societies are social spaces; they are spaces produced and transformed by human life, and they bear the stamp of the collective life of the communities that call that land home. When Australia was colonised by Europeans, the land was transformed for a new society and way of life. This society and way of living is invested in every part of the land; the place we call Australia is synonymous with the European settlers who transformed the landscape to reflect their culture and ways of living. This way of life, the culture, the work, the folklore, the customs, have all shaped the landscape that is synonymous with Australia. The successive transformations, in modern history, of this land and its landscapes bear the stamp of this White Australian culture and way of life. In political debates about origins and natives, the land is invoked as though one could go back to or retrieve this land before it was transformed by European settlement.

In *The production of space*, Henri Lefebvre writes: *"Everyone wants to protect and save nature; nobody wants to stand in the way of an attempt to retrieve its authenticity. Yet at the same time everything conspires to harm it. The fact is that natural space will soon be lost to view. Anyone so inclined may look over their shoulder and see it sinking below the horizon behind us."*

A place takes shape through human habitation and then becomes a site that is inseparable from that human way of life.

Lefebvre says: *"every society produces a space ..., its own space. The city of the ancient world cannot be understood as a collection of people and things in space. ... For the ancient city had its own spatial practice: it forged its own-appropriated-space.*

"... social space 'incorporates' social actions, the actions of subjects both individual and collective who are born and who die, who suffer and who act. From the point of view of these subjects, the behaviour of their space is at once vital and mortal: within it they develop, give expression to themselves, and encounter prohibitions; then they perish, and that same space contains their graves. From the point of view of knowing, social space works as a tool for the analysis of society. To accept this much is at once to eliminate the simplistic model of a one-to-one or 'punctual' correspondence between social actions and social locations, between spatial functions and spatial forms."

The production of the place called Australia, then, was through the settlement of a White society, with the aim of producing a White way of life akin to those in other parts of the world. The work, the culture and the community, socio-politically speaking, had to be White; this whiteness suffused the land, the land was built with the culture and work of the members of this community. In the successive phases of the history of modern Australia, the reproduction of this way of life also constantly put its stamp on the land, taking shape through the land and at the same time transforming the land to be the crucible of the ethno-racial community of whiteness.

This historico-political reality of the socio-spatial is manifested in all work, from the arts to the trades to the professions and education. We see the political needs of this in the life of the community that is considered the Australian people. No doubt the socio-spatial is subject to the changing realities of the global economy, migration, the settlement of new communities and cultures, and the emergence of new forms of work, but one sees through all these changes the evolution and adaptation of the spaces that were fundamental to the White Australian way of life. In other words, the spaces that were cleared in bringing into existence the place called Australia, the Australian community, these spaces that symbolise Australia are at the heart of, or are crucial components of, the life and work of the nation we call Australia. We see these spaces shaping the nature of work and the social spaces even as Australian life and the spaces of social life seem to be changing like never before. It would be a mistake to leave this space, the place called Australia, out of any consideration of work and social life in Australia. Although it would be error to see everything happening in Australia as an outcome of this spatial reality, there is no work or life in Australia that is not shaped by this ethno-racial space Australia. We would be mistaken to see teaching, accounting, construction, welding, or medicine as not deriving from and working towards the perpetuation of this spatial matrix. It may be said that there is much in all types of work and professions that is not connected to the space of the old White Australia; it may be held that many economic activities, for instance in ethnic enclaves, in Australia are today linked to a global economy and its networks. While this may be true, to the extent these forms of work and social life are conducted in Australia, they are subject to the exigencies of the local socio-spatial.

There are elements that escape the controlling forces of the local society, and there are many processes that are changing local social life and spaces; however, the local, in as much as it is a local Australian space, remains linked to the necessities of White Australia's spatial and social logics. To take this out of the analyses that describe the changes we see in Australia is to strip the local of its White racial dynamics, and to insist that social change —be it social or spatial (one and the same, since one happens together with changes to the other)—is corroding the old is to deemphasise how ethno-racial hegemony operates in Australia. To anticipate our arguments, space in Australia is organised towards racial segregation, for the promotion or protection of the forms of life and work that came together with White settlement.

So, we have a society organised towards racial stratification and White hegemony; this organisation is orchestrated through segregation in social life, namely residential segregation, educational segregation, and segregation in work. Ideas about modern society and culture (shaped by notions about the individual, merit, talent, aptitude) militate against seeing segregation as an ongoing political necessity that structures social life and its everyday spaces in Australia. This segregation is the indispensable political element behind maintaining the idea of whiteness as a phenotype, as a numerical force, as a social, cultural and historical norm in Australia.

We will now go on to discussing these ideas about society, produced through institutionalised knowledge but also powerfully influenced by larger social culture. We will attempt to demonstrate how these ideas derive from, interact with, produce and sanctify the lived spaces and places of everyday life—that is homes, work, art, science, and politics in Australia.

Works referred to
1. Saunders, John *Skilled Migration and the Workforce: an Overview* (2008) NCVER
2. Omi, Michael, Winant, Howard *Racial Formation in the United States: From the 1960s to the 1990s*, Routledge (1994)
3. Lefebvre, Henry, *The production of Space* Wiley-Blackwell (1991)

3

The White Norm

What is a social fact? How do social facts come about? How are they produced and organised? And how do they gain currency in social life? Importantly, how do dominant interests shape the creation of social facts? And how do these facts in turn shape and sanctify social life? These are urgent questions in relation to Australia. They are urgent precisely because these questions are decided by interests that create consensus on what matters in society; how we should think and talk about inclusion and/or equality and so on. When we think about these in relation to Australia, we must also think about who speaks for equality, and what their ideas of equality are. Can the voices in the public sphere, or the institutions that promote research and debate represent the varied needs for inclusion and equality in contemporary Australia? In bringing them all under the rubric of a general equality and inclusion, couldn't we ask whose interests are served the best by these general ideas of society, inclusion, and equality? Is this generality devoid of any cultural norm? If there is a cultural norm or a set of norms that shape public debate, couldn't we say that these norms promote certain ideas of the economic and the social?

Do institutions and actors, like the universities, the legal system, and the media, reflect the diversity that we see in wider society? If they represent that diversity in specific ways, or rather if they can only represent that diversity as "minorities", can that have an impact on the nature of the justice, the ideas, knowledge, and debates produced through these institutions? If the presence of these "minorities" in public institutions and in the workforce is the outcome of a social necessity related to organising society towards a majoritarianism and a racial norm that derives from it, couldn't that shape the knowledge and the discourses produced by these institutions about work, about life, and about Australia? In other words, if we see the institutional agenda and/or the national agenda as already decided, and "minorities" as people who must fit into and contribute to this already agreed upon agenda of equality, inclusion, and so on, wouldn't that have an over-determining effect on how we conceive of equality and society? In that case, wouldn't the effects of these discourses produced by institutions, the institutional effects so to speak, limit or determine the scope of social life in decisive ways? Can we make a legitimate distinction between social life, private life and public concerns? Is the nature of the disconnect — i.e., the fact that non-Whites have no presence in Australia's public sphere — between the life of racial minorities, immigrants from the Global South and the public sphere accidental? Or is there a political necessity that manifests itself in the racialised nature of Australia's public sphere?

White intellectuals and social science research

The belief that the personnel and the cultural background of the personnel in an Australian institution cannot have a bearing on its ideas about inclusion and equality, or about culture and society, gives the institutions of public life an aura of neutrality, especially because these institutions claim that equality and inclusion are the very purpose of their social existence. The debates and the usual questioning that is characteristic of much of this work on society lends it an air of concern and representativeness. The presumed neutrality, seemingly emerging through requirements of critique, debate, and review, enables communities of professionals, like writers and researchers, to produce work that shapes agendas, paradigms, and a consensus. Reaching out to or speaking up for "difference" could seem like solidarity, but we rarely think of the political necessities instigating and structuring these forms of solidarity, or if this solidarity can empower those who have no voice. It is hard not to think if this work and solidarity with the "marginalised" is more about enhancing the power and status of those who speak for the "marginalised".

The cultural consensus shaping the political necessities behind institutionalised efforts to understand and empower the "marginalised" in Australia are linked to the majoritarian compulsions structuring the workforce, and its imperatives for knowledge-production that reinforce the racial norm of Australia. In this context we must keep in mind the nationalistic concerns and the institutional matrix that organises the work of writers and scholars. We must also keep in mind the ethno-cultural make-up of the people who compose the community of writers and knowledge workers. All these factors point to the ethno-racial norms and political concerns of the knowledge production and literary culture of Australia. It must not be thought that this norm does not or historically has not enabled concerns about equality or inclusion to be raised within its orbit.

The institutions of Australia are shaped by the cultural life and mores surrounding these institutions, and they have a powerful role in working together in promoting the values based on racial majoritarianism. However, we think of institutions as places that foster professionalism and systematic rational inquiry and debate concerning society, even as we often debate and discuss the work that is done by these institutions. The public sphere of Australia, shaped as it is by the institutions of government and the bureaucracies of the state, gives these social concerns visibility, and through that determines what can legitimately be said about social issues. It also determines the shape and limits of these discussions. It is not that a reigning paradigm cannot have room for differences or variation, but these differences often end up being assimilated into the reigning norm in a process that reinforces social hierarchies and the status quo. This is why we see diversity as an adjunct to the greater transcending concerns about nation, society, work and so on. This place of diversity is reflected not just in the composition and agendas of the literary-intellectual landscape of Australia, it also shows in the way diversity is framed in the public sphere.

Much has been written about paradigms that inform social scientific research and how communities of knowledge workers produce knowledge informed by these paradigms. A paradigm gains hegemony through the adherence of intellectuals, and the problematics it enables them to engage with. These problematics are tied to the ways society thinks of the social world and its concerns. We know how these paradigms are defended and how they endure in time through the routine work of communities of scholars and writers. Often, we hear about the disciplinary boundaries that shape questions of equality or community — like, for instance, economics, sociology, history, anthropology, etc — and how these shape the nature of the knowledge and the limits of the problematics that are tied to disciplines. For our purposes here it is important to remember that ideas of community and equality in Australia are shaped by a larger context of White racial hegemony; it is the needs of this racial hegemony that organises the workforce and the labour market towards its needs for supremacy. An Australian scholar or writer may consider herself to be for equality, but the type of equality they stand for cannot stray far from what the community of whiteness has legitimised as permissible. It is this need for speaking, articulating, and promoting the needs of whiteness in all its shades that organises the workforce and the labour market in all its prestigious sectors and professions. A writer or knowledge worker then is sanctioned through a job/profession to promote the interests of ethno-racial hegemony.

The preceding comments should give an idea of what is meant here by the politics of equality and inclusion in Australia. There are many concerns and interests that converge in ideas of equality in Australia. Some of these are global norms, like universal human rights; others have emerged through the local history of White Australia and its historical efforts to promote whiteness and White privilege through political and social struggles engaged on the terrain of work and the labour force. As mentioned earlier, Australia's history has never been free of protecting White interests, i.e., ethno-racial interests and norms, in all spheres of social life, and it would be hard to see any aspect of social or personal life in Australia that does not bear the stamp of this historical necessity of segregation that enabled a specific political community to emerge and endure in time.

Western society and its ideas of work

It would not be far-fetched to argue that the socio-economic interests of White Australia, i.e., the racial formation called Australia, have historically been synonymous with national welfare and wellbeing. Thus, many current ideas of socio-economic equality are inseparable from Australia's White working-class movements, and the White left that has enormous clout in the institutionalised spaces of Australia. This White left and its ideas of economic redistribution or equality is often considered as a socialist trend (touted as a generalised program of equality that transcends ethno-racial differences), that historically had little to do with White Australia and its agenda of promoting the interests of White workers over other immigrant communities in Australia. It is as if settler colonialism was not formative of Australia's working classes and its organisation of work.

These ideas of equality, that see race/racism as irrational

prejudiced behaviour and discrimination, work towards minimising the omnipresence of racial concerns in the contemporary workplace. Racial welfare and the socio-political anxieties it historically generated are usually couched in ideas of efficiency that derive from ethnocentric histories of Western culture; disguised as national welfare, they come with notions of cultural suitability in the workforce, and with concerns about standards and quality of work—everyday life is suffused with these notions of the superiority of Western products and work practices.

The relocation of manufacturing from Europe, America, and Australia to the Global South is normally associated with large-scale job losses in the Western world. Whether it is job losses or anxiety over China's status as the factory of the world, everyday life and language in Australia are rarely free of concerns about the relocation of manufacturing to the Global South, which is normally associated with Chinese manufacturing and economic activity. It is common to hear comments like "good quality... not made in China" or "cheap Chinese rubbish". Hence it is naïve to think that concerns about globalisation, outsourcing, Australian jobs, and similar sentiments are free of racial anxieties. It is sometimes held that these racial concerns are antithetical to the working class's fundamental interests against an abstract capitalism (abstract as it is free of the ethno-racial). The Australian union movement and the Left generally promote ideas of community that aim for gains to local communities that transcend racial divides. It is as if these supposedly-secular and cosmopolitan movements have managed to reform the socio-racial and keep it at bay. As mentioned previously, ideas of an egalitarian Australia arise from these abstract notions of Left Australia that consider its history as capable of being freed from a profoundly racialised nature and past. The generalised idea of equality current in Australia, the idea of equality that informs research, journalism, and political activism, has historical antecedents in the many varieties of communism and socialism that were White supremacist all through Australia's history. Promoting the rights of White workers and protecting them against Chinese, Indians, Afghans, Melanesians, and Indigenous labour has been a continuing concern of the Australian working-class movement. In the history of Australia, it would be hard to find a phase when Whiteness was conceived apart from its socio-economic moorings. It could be said that it is impossible to be a White human if the economic interests, the economic underpinnings i.e., of whiteness, are corroded.

The concerns related to protecting local workers, in other words protecting jobs that promote the white way of life, are also paramount in debates about immigration and the racial mix in Australia. The material base of whiteness is enshrined in inseparable ways in the system of occupations and work that make up contemporary Australian life. We tend to associate occupations with a universal/global work culture and economy. Hence, the system of occupations based on education, training, skill, and talent are synonymous with our ideas of democratic society, upward mobility through education, and equality and "fairness". However, in Australia, as in other societies of the world, this global occupational structure is subject to the needs and politics of local racial supremacy, which, of course, is based on the global racial hierarchy.

White knowledge and the institutions of whiteness

For some time now we've been hearing a great deal about globalisation and the erosion of national cultures. It is argued that this globalisation is fanning the flames of ethno-cultural chauvinism in the Islamic world, South Asia, and other similar regions of the world. Globalisation is also associated with the rise of xenophobia and racial chauvinism in the Western world. So, we have political movements, allegedly on the fringes of Australian politics, that promote xenophobia in a time of rising multiculturalism and seemingly-embattled Australian ways of living. These movements are often cast as extreme reactions to a changing world. However, these nationalistic socio-political movements, as well as the nationalistic side of all Australian politics and social life, must not be seen as a new phenomenon; rather they are a continuation of historical-cultural patterns of ethno-racial jingoism and xenophobia that are inseparable from Australia as we know it.

Mass immigration and multiculturalism make Australia look like a leader in a world that claims to be for pluralism. But, as mentioned in the introduction, we must not see industrialisation as a historical process that transformed societies like Australia; we must rather see Australia as a society that appropriated industrialisation for its own racial hegemony. Similarly, we must not see globalisation and immigration as transformative in one direction, i.e., as transforming Australian society through changes in its economic and social structure. Rather, we must see White Australia as a racial formation powerful enough to subject changes in the economy and society to its own racial political agenda of aggrandisement and hegemony. This political agenda is inseparable from concerns about the right racial mix in Australia's population. This racial mix is crucial not just in relation to the absolute numbers, but importantly in how these numbers are distributed in society according to the necessities of the socio-racial.

We tend to think of this distribution of the races as contingent, or accidental, or resulting from the circumstances of immigration and settlement. Nothing could be further from the truth about contemporary Australia. From schooling and education, to work, the arts, culture, and residential settlement, this mix in Australia is socially organised in keeping with the politics of racial stratification and privilege.

The preceding remarks are meant to call attention to these powerful racial interests that structure everyday life in Australia; for our purposes it is necessary to see cultural mores and ideas that legitimise the ethno-racial as a neutral or unavoidable social fact as conscious collective socio-political imperatives, in line with dominant racial interests, that also work towards silencing questions about the profoundly racialised nature of everyday life in Australia.

The image of Australia as a White society is not a neutral brute social fact arising from a supposedly White ethnic majority and its history of living on the continent; rather, it is a political program that informs the entire spectrum of individual actions in institutions and everyday social life. It would be simplistic to see White life as a social form outside of the institutions of power, and as unconnected to or removed from the domain of the public arena and social power. This ethno-racial collectivity is inseparable from the institutions and the composition of the institutions. The institutions work to maintain the hegemony of this ethno-racial community through its work of knowledge production, administration, and cultural activities. Life and work in Australia are enmeshed in this socio-political and cultural matrix that promotes White hegemony.

Rather than seeing institutions of government and public life as mediators of social differences, as promoters of social harmony or integration, we could see bureaucracies and state agencies as spaces populated by specific ethno-cultural groups who infuse the institutions of public life with their values and world views on society and history—these are crucial sites for the staging of ethno-racial majoritarianism through work and through institutions that govern and organise work in society. We could argue that the institutions of public life are the institutions of ethno-cultural groups that promote their social mores and world views through these institutions, and in the process create the aura of neutrality and social welfare as their guiding principles.

It is possible, then, to think that the appearance of a consensus on society, to the extent that such a thing is possible, is an ethno-racial norm that then inflects ideas about society, culture, rights, economy, health, and well-being. In other words, ideas and paradigms that shape thinking about society are the outcomes of dominant ethno-racial norms. In the case of Australia, of course, this can be seen as the White norm, or whiteness. Race scholarship is replete with research on the racial nature of knowledge, and how it derives from and so sanitises ethno-racial privilege.

Whiteness as the ethno-racial norm

It is important to bear in mind that an ethno-racial norm, any ethno-racial norm, in a globalised world characterised by mass politics, is not wholly exclusionary or repressive; rather it works through democratic mass politics and bureaucratic structures in ethno-racially diverse national social formations, adapting and accommodating the multiplicity that is characteristic of all societies. In thinking of whiteness, apart from all that has been written about it like the emergence of race and whiteness in modernity, the history of colonialism and slavery, empire and its politics, White nationalism, Eurocentrism, White privilege — we must think of it as a democratic socio-cultural formation in the sense that it is appropriable and lends itself to appropriation by a wide cross-section of cultural groups, in fact by any cultural group. Also, behind what we see as modernity or modern institutions, the White norm is always already at work, being appropriated and adapted to every imaginable ethnic culture or locale. The White norm then is also a global norm that is always being localised everywhere in the world at this historical moment, be it through militant Islam, Arab nationalism, Indigeneity, Hindu nationalism, or Buddhism. In many ways, whiteness is synonymous or is present in all forms of bureaucracy, cultural sophistication, and/or modernity. This makes the workings of organisations, bureaucracies, state agencies, and business practices look neutral or global in Australia. In many ways, the ethno-racial norm of Australia, whiteness, signifies efficiency, ability, modernity, and cosmopolitanism.

What makes us think that equality is a neutral term, and the neutrality of equality can make us transcend or mitigate the divides in a fundamentally-racialised society? Do we equate equality with a post-racial society? Or do we think of equality as a social program that can be on the agenda of a multi-racial society? Can equality and multi-raciality co-exist? Can there be a race-neutral socio-political agenda for co-existence? Who would dictate the terms of this co-existence then? What would the grounds be for this co-existence? In the time of multi-racial societies, can we think of opportunities and resources as neutral? Can we think of political and social programs as race neutral? Or are they the outcome of groups organised as races promoting their own racial interests as social welfare? If it is the case that social welfare is a program that reflects and promotes the interests of hegemonic groups in society, how are these interests organised and promoted? Can we see facts about society as neutral or general if they are the outcome of struggles between ethno-racial groups? If welfare, for example, is neutral and permits diverse sections of society, ethno-racially, to come together, can such multi-racial coalitions be forged on terms of equality? Or is there a norm that necessitates coalitions to come together under certain conditions that are the result of prevailing power relations in society; that is, relations of power tied to the racial hierarchy?

How does the racial hierarchy instrumentalise itself in social life? What if we see the institutions of public life, like the courts, media, the universities, schools, political parties, and activist groups as spaces that enable certain cultural groups to assert their interests, ideas, and norms against other interests? What if we see Australia's courts, universities, media, schools, and bureaucracies that produce knowledge about society as spaces that gather communities of professionals (like writers, lawyers, researchers, and statisticians) to produce work that shapes agendas and paradigms, and through these build a consensus. Couldn't we think of the ethno-racial norm as a norm that is actualised in everyday life and practice through the matrix of institutions that Australian social life is centred around? Can we not, then, think that everyday life and its practices are structured and reproduced through these institutional networks? Can we then afford to think that a medical doctor, journalist, lawyer, professor, schoolteacher, or bureaucrat acts for a neutrality that is intended towards the post-racial? Or do they act in conformity to the needs of racial politics? Can there be a consensus that is not influenced by cultural norms? Can culture, with all its multiplicity and hybridity, be free of economic and political concerns? Can politico-economic concerns be above or beyond the cultural life of communities of people?

We must now look at how the White norm shapes the politics of the labour market, housing, and education in Australia. As mentioned previously, these are three realms that are seen as sites that promote social integration and upward mobility. Contrary to these common conceptions, the argument here is that the labour market, housing, and education are three sites that reproduce and reinforce the racial hierarchy and racial stratification. Integration, like any other social concept, is complex. One of the popular senses of the term is to refer to a society that values equality of opportunity and pluralism in a manner that is race neutral and colour blind. As we discussed earlier, equality, opportunity, and pluralism are all powerfully racialised in Australia, and writing and research conducted with the aim to promote integration promotes the politics of race and the racial status quo.

Immigration and the labour market

The labour market in Australia is discussed by economists and social scientists as an institution that is, in many respects, internal to a society and reflecting its own work ethos and history of labour. However, in the case of the rich immigrant destination nations of North America, ANZ, and western Europe, it would be impossible to overestimate the role immigration plays in shaping the labour market. As discussed earlier, immigration wasn't just an indispensable requirement to socially engineer the Australian labour market; it continues to be a crucial structuring phenomenon of what is considered a rich post-industrial labour market. The transformation in Australia's migration regime from permanent settlement to skilled and temporary labour migration is the latest avatar of this history of social engineering that maintains the whiteness of Australia, brand Australia, through the labour market and immigration. In discussions about migration to Australia, it is common to see periodisations explaining a series of transformations that have characterised the history of migration in Australia. As with other histories, these histories sometimes nostalgically refer to past periods to contrast the "good old days" of migration and settlement in Australia with the troubling aspects of contemporary migration.

The romanticisation of immigration and the immigrant is a powerful feature of settler societies, as many writers have explained. This romanticisation inflects the periodisations that structure contemporary narratives about the crisis facing immigration and settler societies today. The days of permanent settlement, for example, are compared to the current phase characterised by the growth in temporary migration, and this phase is held to be corroding the inclusive values of yesterday. Such analyses emphasise breaks and mutations in history and society that are hard to reconcile with contemporary observations of everyday life. It could just as easily be maintained that, despite the enormity of social transformations today, we still see the traditional social/racial hierarchies and old forms of domination, status, and privilege finding new grounds to flourish in a seemingly-changed Australia. It is then necessary to see these changes as conducive to the perpetuation of older norms in work and social life; as mentioned previously, social analyses have created the impression that these are separate or separable domains.

At the outset it should be mentioned that Australia's immigration program and policies keep changing to adjust to competing demands and realities. What we attempt to discuss here is the role of race and racialised interests through these changing priorities of immigration policy. It should not be thought that race remains an unchanging constant. Rather, race and racial interests remain hegemonic, as in the past, in the present moment. Surely, the changes in society both at the local and global levels work towards transforming racial interests in substantial ways. However, for our argument we need to stress the role of race in structuring a multitude of phenomena under consideration here.

4

Immigration and race neutrality

The following is a discussion of research on immigration and the Australian labour market. The works cited here are a representative sample of certain types of research and the concerns of Australian immigration scholarship. It is also an attempt to show how social science frames our understandings of society, and how this institutionalised effort at systematic rational inquiry and discussion of immigration is rarely free of the larger folk social anxieties and concerns about this problem?

Temporary migration and the labour market

The transformation from a migration regime organised towards permanent settlement to a regime emphasising temporary migration in Australia is a local development of a global dynamic of migration, characterised by increased flows of migrants from the Global South to the north and other affluent societies. Together with goods and services, a vastly increased flow of labour across the globe has ushered in a new era of migration that is distinctly different from the preceding waves of migration in the 20th century. These changes are seen as fundamental transformations to the settler society ethos of Australia, erasing differences between settler societies and other immigrant-receiving nations in Europe, as writers like Catherine Dauvergne have argued.

In this context, it is useful to stress the global nature of this phenomenon. As Khalid Koser says, migration is an important aspect of the global economy, and is "embedded" in the transformations of the global economy and society. Increasing levels of demographic and developmental disparities trigger the movement of large populations across the globe. The segmentation of the labour market in the rich migrant destination societies and the jobs crisis in the Global South together propel the current waves of immigration.

Similarly, Anna Boucher and Lucie Cerna say that many features of labour immigration patterns and policies are peculiar to the contemporary period: firstly, immigration is overwhelmingly economic in focus today; and secondly, there is a strong emphasis on temporary economic immigration, although these forms can become permanent over time. Boucher and Cerna say that although immigrant destination nations need a variety of immigrants across the skill spectrum, governments tend to emphasise and prioritise "skilled immigrants". So, the global race for talent, and the need to stay competitive economically, plus the demographics of the global village (ageing populations in the destination nations vs a restless and youthful population in the Global South), make up the factors determining the nature of immigration today.

Accordingly, in Australia, dramatic increases in immigration levels in the last two decades are being driven primarily by skill stream visa grants, which increased from about 24,000 in 1996 to about 128,000 in 2015. The share of skill stream immigrants in the migration program increased from about 29 per cent in 1996 to about 68 per cent in 2015. For our purposes, the dichotomy skilled/unskilled is crucial.

Discussing the concept of skill, Boucher and Cerna explain that labour migration "needs to be thought through a division between 'skilled' and 'unskilled' entry. High skilled migrants are defined as those with tertiary-level education, and low-skilled migrants are those who have primary education". Although tertiary education is often a necessary qualification for a visa for "high skilled migrants", "highly educated" is not equivalent to "highly skilled". However, they say, in the future most migrants entering the OECD will be "skilled".

The shift in Australia from permanent settlement to temporary migration has been extensively discussed. Its impacts on the labour market and other areas of society have been dominant concerns of public discussion, even when these changes are not understood well or explicitly discussed as such.

Briefly, the story is something like this: In the mid-1940s, Australia gradually opened its doors to immigrants from countries other than Britain and Ireland. From the 1960s to the 1970s, the White Australia policy was gradually dismantled, and, starting in the mid-1980s, increasing priority was given to skilled migration. Soon, skilled migrants made up most of the permanent migrant intake. Permanent settlement made up a crucial component of

Australia's post-war population policy. Australia's contemporary image of a settler society was built upon waves of permanent migrants. Today, however, most migrants coming into Australia at any point in time are here on temporary visas.

However, migration levels have not remained the same in the last 60 years (the period we are considering). In periods of economic downturn, migration levels dropped. A pattern emerged, according to Andrew Markus, James Jupp and Peter McDonald, in which migration levels were high in good times and low in periods of economic recession. In the 1980s, when migration from the Global South started increasing dramatically, net migration rose to record levels and then plummeted following the recession in the 1990s. Many immigrants who arrived in the late 1990s were not able to find jobs. This situation contributed to the development of the points system, whereby immigrants were awarded points for qualifications, work experience, age, and English proficiency. Not long after this, a further shift in policy initiated large-scale temporary migration to deal with shortages in the labour market.

Coinciding with these shifting priorities of the state and policy is the rising numbers of immigrants from Asia. The "Asianisation" of migration was well underway, and so were the structural features of the segmented labour market that we see today.

We must note here the important points for our argument: the first one is the growth in skilled migration, and the next one is the dramatic increase in temporary migrants to Australia, the majority being skilled migrants—where skilled migrant is a category that encompasses a wide variety of younger and economically active immigrants. Labour migration is the defining feature of the latest waves of migration, not just in Australia but in all immigrant destinations. We must now try to see how this immense demographic transformation wrought by immigration has structured the labour market, and how research and the public sphere veils this changed reality with a race-neutral discussion on jobs and the economy.

In thinking of the labour market and its role in reproducing the racial hierarchy, we must ask how this trend of increasing labour migration and the mix of high-skilled and low-skilled manifests in Australia; the emergence of these global realities in Australia, we must bear in mind, can never be understood apart from the realities of the public sphere and the voices that animate the debates about migration. Who speaks for the migrant and immigration in the public sphere, and what the institutional, political, and cultural interests of these voices are is indispensable in understanding the interests that manage immigration flows into Australia. This is to say that our understanding of immigration today is shaped by the media and scholarly writing about immigration. These voices promote the White norm even as they champion the cause of immigration and multiculturalism.

What is the place of the credentialled "educated" and "highly skilled" immigrant from the Global South in Australia's labour market? Does the labour market recognise credentials from the Global South? If so, how? If not, why not? Could we say that, so far as the immigrant from the Global South goes, credentials are not of any great value in the Australian labour market? Could we say that ethnicity/race/nationality dominates over credentials and professional background or suitability in Australia? We cannot cursorily pass over these questions if we want to understand the "function" of the labour market in maintaining the socio-racial. Nor can we afford to rest content with the answers and explanations proffered by migration scholars and other observers.

Discussing the shift from permanent settlement to temporary migration in Australia, Robert G Gregory, in the paper *The two-step Australian immigration policy* and its impact on immigrant employment outcomes, says that while formerly, immigrants to Australia came as permanent settlers with the right to work, today, temporary visa holders with work entitlements outnumber permanent settler visas by a "ratio of three to one". This new situation with large numbers of temporary visa holders, in Gregory's view, has led to a two-step immigration policy whereby many migrants enter the country initially as temporary residents, mostly as international students, and then attain permanent residency. About one half of permanent visas are granted on-shore to those on temporary visas with work rights. Immigrants from non-English speaking countries are the most impacted by this two-step system. In their initial years they report "substantially reduced full-time employment and substantially increased part-time employment". Even three years after arrival, one-third of immigrants from a non-English speaking background are in part-time employment. However, immigrants from English speaking countries continue to report better labour market outcomes.

This, then, is our problem, or rather the symptom of the problem we are trying to elaborate: A changing labour market that claims to need "highly skilled" workers; the largest number of these "highly skilled" workers pouring in from Asia/ the Global South, and the labour market distributing them according to demand/needs or phenotype. We must not expect any straightforward, easy, or conclusive answers. Examining a sample of the research on this matter gives us insights into the race-neutral nature of the debate on immigration, and what this colour-blind research attempts to veil or leave in silence.

How the colourblind researcher weighs in

Labour market economists, migration scholars, and other social scientists are called upon regularly to assess the impact immigration has on the domestic labour force. A good deal of social science research today is dedicated solely to producing data on this matter, and, as with any data, the political climate shapes the nature of the questions and the "facts" they generate. Research attempts to decide if immigrants are taking jobs that should go to locals, and if immigration has an impact on the wages of locals, for instance, or if the concentration of immigrants in particular industries tends to depress wages and deteriorate working conditions in these sectors. Social science attempts to answer community concerns about jobs, the conditions of work, and the other socio-cultural impacts immigration has on Australian society. The charged nature of the debate and the way it is framed in the public sphere shapes social science inquiry and the data. The anxiety about Australian jobs or Australian culture are always the background, i.e., the socio-political context, of this research.

It is impossible to say where one issue/concern ends, and other anxieties begin; if jobs can be separated from ethno-culture? And, if so, how? To what extent, for example, can native/domestic worker be separated from race/ethnicity? So, while "liberal" or "progressive" observers may focus on employment and unemployment of locals and overseas-born workers, on the types of jobs immigrants do, and if these jobs are in sectors faced with labour shortages, and while their research may "confirm" that immigration delivers net gains to Australia, much of this analyses functions as coded colourblind language that obfuscates the racial imperatives of the labour market. This is to say that research framed through economistic or similar paradigms, that strip out the race factor, or view it as the problem of language, culture, or ethnicity, ends up deemphasising the segmentation of the labour market and how a segmented labour market functions towards reproducing and reinforcing the racial hierarchy.

Discussing the impact of immigration on the labour market, the Productivity Commission's *Migrant Intake into Australia Productivity Commission (PC) Inquiry Report No 77 2016* says: *"The costs of immigrants reaching their potential — notably those costs that are borne by Australian taxpayers — need to be factored into any assessment of immigration. And while immigration may be beneficial for the economy as a whole, the net benefits of immigration may not be evenly shared, so distributional consequences need to be assessed".* This sentence reflects the ambivalent tone of much research in Australia when it comes to discussing the impact of immigration on local jobs; there is no debate on the necessity or overall good of immigration or diversity; however, its adverse impacts need to be understood "scientifically". As mentioned earlier, research echoes the economic concern of the community on immigration, and such concerns are a combination of anxieties, even when they come packaged as economics. Couched in economic or social scientific language, the framing of the issue in this manner puts the onus on immigration to prove its benefits to the local community. It is known that immigrants are not beneficiaries of social spending, especially in their early years in Australia, yet the question is asked about the financial cost of newcomers to the community. Also, the biggest group of immigrants, including permanent and temporary immigrants, are skilled labour migrants. The Australian Bureau of Statistics says that in the year 2016-2017 (for example) the income tax contribution of immigrants to Australia was $112 billion out of $550 billion total income tax collected.**

The PC report acknowledges that the common conception of immigrants taking local jobs is based on the mistaken notion of a fixed number of jobs in the economy (the lump of labour fallacy), and this leads to the belief that any new arrival takes a job that should have gone to a local. The report says that minimum wages and penalty rates add complexity to the analysis of immigration on the local labour force. It grants that immigrants not just add to the local supply of labour but, through their spending, raise the demand for labour and complement existing skills in the labour force. The report says that the "overall effect on locals' wages and unemployment from immigration is an empirical matter". However, the effects of immigration on the labour market may be difficult to disentangle, and among the reasons cited are the fact that the labour market is heterogenous, and a simple demand

and equilibrium model is insufficient to account for the disparate tendencies of the market.

Despite this seemingly-balanced approach, the PC argues that immigration may not cause unemployment at the aggregate level, but it may hurt the prospects of those workers in sectors with "high concentrations of immigrants".

"Many Australian nurses, recent graduates and older people, see themselves as being displaced by imported nurses and they and their families, who depend on them, [are] impoverished. Even unions, which tend to be pro-migrant, have been forced to represent their members on this matter. ... I have also gained the impression that hospitals are teaming up with universities to import nurses on the understanding that they will enrol for higher degrees at local universities, whilst employed. Does the public benefit, or is this really a credentialing bonanza for hospitals and universities. Local nurses must then compete by paying for more training at inflated prices, but with deflated employment opportunities."

Notice in the above paragraph how impressions reflecting community anxieties are imported into a public document meant to discuss the evidence on the matter of immigration and its impact on the local job market. This is an example of the porousness of research, the permeability of its borders with community sentiments that are thinly-disguised xenophobia. Are there any empirical grounds to believe Australian unions, or organised labour movements anywhere in the world, are pro-immigration? How can we believe that unions representing Australian workers are free of anxieties stemming from immigration, and the concurrent demographic changes? How can we think that the labour force is not structured by the compulsions of majoritarianism that are tied to a community's income and wealth? How could we think that economic competition and conflict are not being disguised as neutral and rational science by a public body producing an ostensibly neutral scientific/economic document? It needs to be mentioned here that research has pointed out that immigrant nurses from the Global South, although performing well in the labour market, lag behind domestic nurses and immigrant nurses from the UK in labour force outcomes.

The PC report then acknowledges the limitations of studies done in the past, and the limitations of any attempt to decide this matter one way or the other. It then goes on to a more recent study based on econometric analyses. The study uses two data sets: HILDA 2001-2014 data on wages matched to Census data from 2001-2011 for immigrant shares by experience/education, and the ABS' Survey of Income and Housing from 2003-04 to 2011-12.

The PC then states its conclusions: *"First, immigrants flow into skill groups with the highest earnings and the lowest unemployment. This is consistent with immigrants coming to Australia with knowledge of those occupations with relatively high returns and with the design and intent of Australia's selective migration policies.*

"Second, once immigrants' movement into skills groups with high wages and/or good labour market conditions are controlled for, the results differ depending on the choice of comparison group and the definition of skill group used.

"The authors conclude that, when taken together, these findings suggest the labour market outcomes (wages, participation and employment) of the

existing Australian community have been neither helped or [sic] harmed by immigration over the period 2000 to 2011 — a period of robust economic growth. However, negligible effects in aggregate are not a reason to assume the presence of negligible effects on certain sub-groups."

As mentioned previously, the conclusions are ambiguous. Given the methodology and the problems inherent in this, as the discussion points out, this is not surprising. However, leaving aside such economic analyses, is there reason to believe immigrants are hurting the job prospects of locals? Or, given our argument about the racial caste system of Australia structuring the labour market, shouldn't we ask if there is evidence of any trends in immigrants displacing locals in well remunerated jobs? Are immigrants generally in well-paying stable professional or para-professional positions? Or are they concentrated in sectors like retail, transport, construction, health care, security/facilities management, and cleaning, that rely on a casualised labour force? In sectors like health care, where immigrants make up high numbers of the workforce, is there evidence that their presence has reduced wages? Are they in these sectors solely for the high wages and relatively good working conditions? Or are the shortages in this sector, Australia's largest employer, creating the need for immigrants with relevant skills and qualifications?

Given the charged nature of the debate and these concerns, it shouldn't surprise that there couldn't possibly be any definitive answers to these questions. Migration research may look at the matter from within the confines of a discipline, even while most people know well that these matters are inextricably tied to change, community, and power in society.

White and non-White workers

Let us now bring into this discussion the problem of race, and the labour force outcomes of White and non-White immigrants. It is generally believed that immigrants struggle to find their place in a new society, especially if there are language and cultural barriers. Historically, immigrants to settler societies like Australia were concentrated in working-class jobs. The post-war manufacturing boom relied, in many Western societies, on large waves of immigration. The settlement patterns in urban areas too reflect this close connection of migrant communities to construction and manufacturing. Often, in everyday life, immigration today is compared to immigration in previous decades, although the circumstances are vastly different. The official history of migration, of European communities to Australia, is sometimes used to make sense of migration today, or judge contemporary migrants. The story of the immigration of Greeks or Italians to Australia is held to be exemplary. It is said that many European communities were seen as aliens or racial Others, and they had to face the same obstacles that migrants today face in the labour market. This discourse of immigration has a powerful hold on the public imagination, and shapes the contemporary immigrant's ideas about Australia as well as their self-understandings of their aspirations. It is almost as if an Indian or Chinese could become like a White European, with time...

While marginalisation and downward mobility may be characteristic for large groups of immigrants from Asia or Europe, the details of this marginalisation and the specific nature of their eventual integration into the "host" society (a White society) is important. The integration of non-Anglo Celtic "White" immigrants and non-White immigrants from Asia may show patterns of marginalisation or labour market segmentation that may be relevant in considerations of contemporary society. It needs to be kept in mind that, in the formation of modern multicultural Australia, this integration of previous generations of immigrants rarely strayed far from the racial divides and ethnic markers that make society what it is today. We could say, against those who champion a past golden age of migration, that the seeds of modern racism and the racial divides of the labour market and settlement patterns we see in Australia today were sown in the 1960s, '70s, and '80s, and these, in turn, were a continuation of historical patterns of racial formation. This is just to say that in general terms there may be plenty of inspiring stories from the so-called golden years of migration to Australia, yet this golden age discourse is another way of silencing and covering over the racial politics of White Australia, and the experiences of the several non-White communities that settled in Australia at the time.

As mentioned, skilled labour migration makes up the bulk of immigration into Australia, be it in the temporary or permanent categories. However, this is also a matter of categorisation, as skill is usually defined as post-school qualifications, and increasing numbers of youth in the migrant source countries have these qualifications. Australia's skilled migration intake is based officially on the assumption that a booming economy is faced with skill shortages, and immigrants selected based on their skills (education and professional experience) will fill these shortages.

Comparing the labour force outcomes of skilled immigrants from Main English Speaking Countries (MESC) to those from Non-English Speaking Countries (NESC), Bob Birrell writes in a 2008 paper *How are skilled migrants doing?* that the MESC group had outcomes similar to those of Australians with degree level qualifications: a majority were employed in professional or managerial positions by 2006. It was the opposite for NESC migrants with professional qualifications. Despite demand for the professions they were qualified in, most of them were unable to find jobs matching their qualifications. The majority of the NESC immigrants at the time earned their qualifications in Australian universities. Birrell concedes that there is ample anecdotal evidence of discrimination in the labour market. However, he says that this discrimination is not directed at their place of birth or culture but possibly their lack of English skills: "there is a large body of evidence showing that migrants with professional qualifications from Non-English-Speaking Countries (NESC) have, in the past, struggled to find professional employment in Australia. Various factors appear to be involved, including training and experience which is not relevant to Australian employers' needs. Many of these migrants also have not possessed the English language communication skills required for professional practice in Australia".

If so, the question arises: how did they graduate in Australia with below-par English skills?

It should be noted here that both groups of NESC immigrants, i.e., those selected offshore and onshore, report poor labour force outcomes, although one group has professional experience and qualifications from their source countries, and the younger group selected onshore have Australian qualifications.

In the paper Immigration Overshoot (2012) Bob Birrell and Ernest Healy attribute the labour force outcomes of immigrants from the Global South to lack of English language ability and local work experience. Birrell and Healy leave out of their discussion the labour market outcomes of non-White immigrants from New Zealand who speak English. These are aligned with sectors that are identified with non-White immigrants.

Birrell and Healy look at the labour force outcomes of accountants, the largest single professional occupational group of migrants attracted to Australia in the first decade of the 2000s. Looking at the evidence, they conclude that there is strong employer demand for MESC-born and Australia-born accountants. Eighty per cent of these, in the 20-29 and 30-64 age groups, were employed as managers or professionals; 68 per cent of the Australia-born were employed as accountants. For the NESC immigrant group, only 43 per cent of the 30- 64-year-old group and 25 per cent of the 20- 29-year-old group were employed as accountants.

Looking at the trade situation of immigrants with Certificate III and IV level qualifications, the paper says that immigrants with a degree level qualification from NESC birthplaces dominated migrant streams into Australia, but only 45 per cent of trade-qualified immigrants were from NESC birthplaces. However, the job outcomes of the Certificate III and IV level group are similar to outcomes for the degree qualified group, i.e., the certificate groups from MESC birthplaces do better in finding positions as technicians or trades workers, or as managers or professionals, than do their counterparts from NESC birthplaces.

Importantly, for our argument here, Birrell and Healy say that trade-qualified cooks who arrived in Australia between 2001 and 2006, although relatively small, report good labour force outcomes, reflecting the demand for cooks in Australia.

It is known that the demand for cooks is related to the racial/ethnic segmentation of the labour market, since large numbers of small businesses are in ethnic enclaves and restaurants, and these in turn play a role in structuring the labour market and driving what is seen as self-propelling "chain migration" processes (an ethnic migrant community with sufficient numbers and a foothold in the host country bringing or creating opportunities for more co-ethnics to migrate to the same destination). Couldn't we legitimately ask if the segmented labour market is determining the distribution of migrants based on phenotype and/or culture? If this seems to be the case, or if there is reason to think that the labour market, given the widespread nature of discrimination, is organised along the lines of a racial divide wouldn't this provide support to the arguments put forward by students of migration that the segmentation of the labour market is creating demand for labour as much as the so-called knowledge economy and its needs for highly skilled professionals? Couldn't we say that the labour market segmented along the lines of race/ethnicity determines the distribution of highly skilled knowledge workers just as much as it determines the distribution of blue-collar workers? If phenotype is a consideration, if phenotype and/or a culture associated with phenotype is playing a role in the workings of the labour market, couldn't we think that work itself is subject to the needs of a ritualistic economy organised around phenotype and its aggrandisement? Couldn't we say that income streams tied to jobs and professions are hijacked by systems of education and credentialling in a process that promotes the value of whiteness in the economy and the labour market?

We cannot remain within the confines of a narrow nationalistic migration scholarship if we want to understand the changing dynamics of globalisation and the transnational processes of labour migration and community formation today. If we accept the terms of the debate, the paradigm that keeps the migration scholar ensconced in her/his ivory tower, we will remain blind to the larger social processes unfolding around us in contemporary society.

The 'White noose'*: The non-White 'professional' in the White labour market

In a 2018 paper *Australia's Skilled Migration Program: Scarce Skills Not Required*, Birrell writes, based on the 2016 census, that most immigrants recently arrived from NESCs cannot find professional jobs. A large number (256,504) of recently arrived overseas-born persons held degree or above level qualifications at the time of the Census. The majority (84%) came from NESCs. Only 24 per cent of the NESC group were employed as professionals as of 2016, compared with 50 per cent of the MESCs and 58 per cent of the same-aged Australian-born graduates.

The paper's findings are that the Skill Stream is recruiting permanent migrants with skilled occupations, by far the largest share of which are professionals. Birrell rejects the idea that the program is designed to fill skill shortages in Australia's labour market. Supporting this argument is the finding that only a small proportion of recently-arrived migrant professionals are actually employed in professional positions; the selection system does not prioritise professional occupations faced with skill shortages and, as a result, is delivering large numbers of professionals in fields that are currently oversupplied, including accounting, engineering, and many of the health professional fields. The paper refutes the government's claim that immigrant skills might be needed in the future, and states that Australia is awash with graduates from both domestic and migrant sources.

The paper asks why the Skilled Independent Category attracts professionals from the Global South to Australia, when the employment prospects for the largest applicant occupations like engineering and accounting are poor. "The reason is that there is a huge pool of professionals in Asia who would like to move a country [sic] with Australia's salary levels and quality of life. ... What this means is that recruitment to the Skilled Independent Category of the Skill Stream is being driven by migrant demand, not Australia's skill needs."

So, the state designs a program intending to attract skilled migrants who will find Australia's high standards of living and better wages enticing. Migration scholars spill a great deal of ink analysing the reasons why immigration policy and outcomes diverge. Ostensibly designed to fill shortages in high skilled occupations, the skilled migration program ends up diverting immigrants to low-skill sectors of the labour market. Is there an invisible hand prompting the labour market? Or is it the needs of the racial caste order of Australia? How can this be explained? Is it the poor English language skills of immigrants? Or is it discrimination by individual employers that leads to most non-White immigrants ending up in specific sectors of the labour market? If English skills are a requirement, how can we explain the presence of non-English speakers, who are not fluent in the language, in jobs that require "competence" in the language? Further, how do workers with poor English skills manage to work in warehouses, factories, construction sites, kitchens, public transport, aged care, and hospitals with colleagues who speak only English, and where the only common language for the business is English? Is English not the language of business in these sectors? Or are there sectors composed of jobs requiring little competence in English? Are there different standards of competence in English for non-native English-speaking White Europeans and non-Whites? How does one determine competence in speech, comprehension, and writing in relation to a job?

To better understand the role of race in structuring the labour market, we must consider both permanent migration and the shift to temporary migration in Australia. Before we look at temporary migration, let's look at other research on the labour market outcomes of immigrants from Asia.

Discussing skilled migration from India to Australia in the decade to 2018, Lesleyanne Hawthorne writes that, although Indian migrants are mostly young and hold post-school qualifications, they face significant challenges in the labour market. The reasons: many have qualified in Australia in oversupplied fields (IT, business/commerce, and accounting). Besides, the spike in migration from India in this period was driven by the IT sector, rendering them vulnerable to downturns.

Val Colic-Peisker, in *'Ethnics' and 'Anglos' in the Labour Force: Advancing Australia Fair?* compares employment outcomes for professionally qualified immigrants from a variety of "birthplaces".

Colic-Peisker writes that there is reason to believe in the "hierarchy" of immigrant groups in the employment market, and that birthplace is far from being a neutral factor in the Australian multicultural workforce "in the first decade of the twenty-first century".

The research discussed so far is about professional roles and/or jobs in the organised sector. However, the segmentation of the labour market should be seen as something that spans across the formal and informal sectors, and this segmented labour market distributes White workers in the formal sector, with good jobs, better pay and conditions, and non-White workers in the informal sectors and/or jobs that are less prestigious or financially rewarding. This segmentation enables White work and jobs to be segregated from the less-rewarding but dirty, dangerous, and demeaning work (3D jobs). We will discuss this again briefly in the chapters on housing and space, and demonstrate how these segmented labour markets are tied to segregated residential areas enmeshing work and personal life through spaces that are carved along the lines of race and ethnicity. It is in this manner that race/racism produces its own segregated spaces, and these segregated spaces should be seen as coded and over-coded with the customs and conventions (work, the arts and culture, love, friendship, neighbourhood, and the spaces of leisure and recreation) of communities of races/ethnicities.

Works referred to

*   See Robert O. Self, American Babylon: *Race and the struggle for post-war Oakland* (2005). Self writes, "The suburban 'white noose' surrounding the urban black community stood metaphorically for urban inequality and segregation".
    A similar argument can be made about the urban labour market for the skilled migrant from the third world in Australia.

**   https://www.abs.gov.au/statistics/people/people-and-communities/personal-income-migrants-australia/latest-release

1. Dauvergne, Catherine. 2016. *The new politics of immigration and the end of settler societies*, Cambridge University Press.
2. Koser, K. 2016. *International migration: A very short introduction*. Oxford University Press.
3. Markus, Andrew *Australian Race Relations: 1788-1993* (Australian Experience). 1994. Allen & Unwin.
4. Money, Jeannette, Lockhart, Sarah P. 2021. *Introduction to International Migration: Population Movements in the 21st Century*, Routledge.
5. Productivity Commission Inquiry Report. 2016. *Migrant intake report* (Also see: *A History of Department of Immigration: Managing migration to Australia* (2015) https://www.homeaffairs.gov.au/about-us-subsite/files/immigration-history.pdf)
6. Wright, Chris F., Clibborn, Stephen. 2020. *A guest-worker state? The declining power agency of migrant labour in Australia*, Labour Relations Review.
7. *Continuous Survey of Australia's Migrants Cohort 6 Report — Introductory Survey 2018*
8. Thomson, Lisa. 2014. *Migrant Employment Patterns in Australia: post Second World War to present* AMES Research and Policy Unit
9. Birrell, Bob, Healy, Ernst, *Immigration Overshoot*, Centre for Population and Urban Research (2012)
10. Colic-Peisker, Val *Employment success of skilled and professional NESB migrants: the most important measures of Australian multiculturalism* Joint Standing Committee on Migration (2011)
11. Hawthorne, Lesleyanne. 2018. *The Recent Transformation of Indian Skilled Migration to Australia*, Aii Discussion Paper 1801.

5
Racial caste and opportunity hoarding

In exposing the workings of the labour market on the lines of race, the researchers we've discussed so far also show how our conception of the labour market is based on that of an integrated pluralistic society: immigration, settlement, labour market participation rates, and so on leading to something like a post-racial society where qualifications, skills, ability, work ethic, business efficiency, entrepreneurship, and similar virtues shape the labour market. In some ways such hopes are not unfounded: work brings together all the races of Australia in complex ways that seem to be promoting integration. Yet, even if the actual day-to-day appearances of working together — for instance an Indian cab driver driving Anglo CEOs and other professionals like a White professor or journalist headed to a ministerial consultation; or an Asian takeaway or laundromat in a White suburb — may be viewed as productive social interaction, the integratory impulse in these situations is more towards a social order centred around a racial caste system and the dependencies that are inherent in this order.

It is this caste system that determines the distribution of the races in Australia's labour market, despite the appearance of diversity within the professions and other occupations. Social science and its ideas of society and work give rise to the belief that it is a loss to society that a cab driver with post-school credentials faces impediments in making use of his/her education in the workforce. And this concern also facilitates the smattering of diversity within white-collar occupations monopolised by White Australians. To the casual observer, this predominance of specific groups of races within segments of the labour market may look like an outcome of skills and credentials; and not the belief that Australia is a White society. In everyday life we always hear comments like "there is little diversity in this organisation" or that certain professions or organisations are mostly White, or that Indians or Asians have cornered certain niches within sectors like retail or transport: we rarely think of this as a structural fact of society, which is the distribution of occupations among the races, and the social closures this trend is based upon.

This is because the distribution of workers in the labour market is considered an outcome of education, aptitude, skills, culture, and networks, and surely there are facts and trends to support these beliefs. These perceptions are also in keeping with contemporary ideas of democracy, upward mobility, and equal opportunity; one's ethnicity or ancestry does not matter so much as the ability to do a job, backed by the required credentials for the job. Employers need skills for their businesses, and whoever can deliver the goods is employable.

Such ideas are oblivious to the vast literature on contemporary work and the labour force that shed important insights into the system of training, mass education, higher education, credentialling, jobs, and the professions, and how all these maintain and reproduce traditional social hierarchies. We tend to think that education and credentialling are required for jobs in a modern knowledge economy allegedly reliant on specialised "high-skilled" workers. This belief is usually unquestioning and is a central trope of modern society: education, training, jobs, upward mobility, talent, vocation, career, and achievement. However, the connection between mass education, higher education, and upward mobility has been shown to be problematic by several researchers.

Writing about the *Literacy Myth*, Harvey Graff questions the belief that literacy leads to upward mobility and the overcoming of inequalities and limitations rooted in racial, ethnic, and gender differences. Graff says that contrary to the widely-held belief that individual achievement may reduce the effects of social inequalities, there is evidence to think that literacy has been used to foster social and political repression.

Researchers argue that the common notion that higher education leads to high incomes and good jobs is mostly unfounded, as highly-paying jobs are mostly clustered in the top tiers, and the earnings of graduates as a whole give little reason to believe that higher education leads to higher incomes. Much of the emphasis in the higher education curriculum is not necessitated by the skills required in the job market. In technological fields, for example, there is an oversupply of graduates, and the job market is unlikely to be able to absorb the rising numbers of qualified professionals. Several studies point to growth in the lowest quartile earning making up nearly half the growth in jobs in the future. Many of these jobs are in hospitality, retail, and health. Many jobs, new and traditional, require little formal training or qualifications. When we think of artificial intelligence and its impact on the labour market, there is reason to think that existing disparities will worsen.

However, the expansion of primary and tertiary education together with vocational education makes education's role in society seem paramount. We should ask how education in Australia maintains its significance in society and the economy. When we consider how Australia's higher education sector has come to rely on and exploit migration from the Global South, or the role of schools in Australia in maintaining ethno-racial segregation and class inequalities, shouldn't we see education and credentialling as pivotal to the system of racial caste and its ritual order in Australia?

US sociologist Randall Collins is one among many who have argued that education cannot be considered the basis of technical skills, but it serves as a means by which opportunities to practice particular forms of work are monopolised, and hence a basis *for restricting access to the actual on-job acquisition of skills*. This point is crucial while considering the distribution of immigrants from the Global South in the Australian labour force in comparison to Australian workers and immigrants from Europe, particularly North-Western Europe.

The credential society

In his 1979 book *The Credential Society*, Randall Collins critiques contemporary myths around mass education and its necessity and role in the labour market. Collins's analysis starts with the idea of the emergence of industrial society from the application of scientific advances to new forms of technology. This creates a perceived need for higher levels of educational attainment, and this in turn changes the requirements for work in contemporary society.

Collins cites research showing that educational requirements for jobs have changed over time, and he writes that it is not clear what the changes in "requirements" mean, as there is little evidence to show what education is really required in jobs today. The case for education is usually made, according to Collins, through the requirements employers have set for jobs at different periods.

"The explanation for these trends has commonly been treated as obvious: Education prepares students in the skills necessary for work, and skills are the main determinant of occupational success. That is, the hierarchy of educational attainment is assumed to be a hierarchy of skills, and the hierarchy of jobs is assumed to be another such skill hierarchy. Hence education determines success, and all the more so as the modern economy allegedly shifts toward an increasing predominance of highly skilled positions."

It is striking how these words resonate with the ideologies about education, skills and work in the Australian labour force. The argument that skilled jobs requiring post-school qualifications are on the rise in Australia is backed by data; however, there is hardly any research that has looked closely at the statistical snapshot bolstering claims about the knowledge economy and the rise in professional occupations.

For instance, we are told that most of the growth in the

labour market in Australia is in professional occupations. This, of course, depends on the definition of "professional", and the criteria used to categorise sectors and the types of jobs within the sectors. We know that the educational level of Australians is on the rise, and nearly half the population has post-school qualifications. There is little research to show if the rising levels of education in the Australian population corresponds to the skill requirements in the labour market, especially for "professional" jobs. Do these jobs require educational credentials or can the skills in a "professional" job be learned on the job? Whatever the case, does the job market and the education sector function according to demand and supply? If so, how does the education sector provide the job market with the skills it requires? If most jobs require skills that can be learned on the job, are there other factors like culture, ethnicity, or networks that trump educational qualifications?

The Australian and New Zealand Standard Classification of Occupations (ANZSCO) defines professional: *"Professionals perform analytical, conceptual and creative tasks through the application of theoretical knowledge and experience in the fields of the arts, media, business, design, engineering, the physical and life sciences, transport, education, health, information and communication technology, the law, social sciences and social welfare."*

And on the requirements for a professional job in Australia:

Bachelor degree or higher qualification. At least five years of relevant experience may substitute for the formal qualification (ANZSCO Skill Level 1); or

AQF Associate Degree, Advanced Diploma or Diploma, or at least three years of relevant experience (ANZSCO Skill Level 2).

Notice how five years of relevant experience may substitute for a formal qualification. This requirement applies to most jobs classified as professional. Since a great number of professions are practised within organisations, this aspect of professionalism is crucial to our argument on the function of the labour market in reproducing the racial hierarchy: on-the-job training and credentialling is a way of opportunity hoarding that ensures the right racial mix prevails in the labour market. The nature of most jobs, the fact that the tasks in a job or occupation can be mastered through experience, facilitates this process, and helps in diminishing the value of credentials from the third world.

The credentials of phenotype

In *The Credential Society*, Collins writes on the career processes within organisations: *"Detailed evidence on the processes of organizational careers shows the overwhelming importance of both informal ties and the struggle to control positions. Studies of promotion patterns show a prevailing pattern of personal sponsorship, whether within industrial organizations, medical careers, or trade union bureaucracies. It is because of the importance of personal acceptability to the sponsoring official and group that ethnic background, old school ties, and club memberships are important in careers. Ethnic distinctions among positions have been pervasive in American industry.*

"Even where there are formal tests and evaluations, as in military promotions, often combined with formal rules of 'up or out' by certain ages or time in grade, informal connections are crucial in acquiring the kinds of assignments that bring an individual to the attention of superiors and provide the background considered appropriate for promotion. In industrial

organizations as well, informal connections are crucial in assignment to those positions that allow horizontal movement and in avoiding too specialized dead-end jobs. The key to success, in other words, has little to do with skilled performance per se, but rather with maneuvring to reach the sequence of positions that lead upward."

None of this is new, and race scholarship has had much to say about these processes of opportunity hoarding in the job force. However, Collins cites research demonstrating that education is central to economic stratification, although it is not the basis of technical skills, but it serves as a means by which opportunities to practice particular forms of work are monopolised, and hence a basis for restricting access to the actual on-job acquisition of skills. According to this argument, highly credentialised professions are the epitome of modern stratification.

Most pertinent to the argument here is Collins' comment about Bourdieu's concept of cultural capital. Schematically speaking, this argument is about how education serves to reproduce class relations in capitalism. Discussing the reproduction of class privileges through a meritocratic educational system, Collins writes that the older system of direct inheritance of material property has been supplanted by a system of indirect material inheritance through the direct inheritance and investment of cultural property.

This is an important point for our purpose to understand the workings of Australia's racial caste system, with the important addition of material inheritance too, in the form of real estate and related wealth. So, we must think of Australia's caste system as a system of both direct and indirect inheritance of material and cultural property. We need to see the direct and indirect forms of inheritance as inextricably enmeshed in a system that creates privileges deeply rooted in ethno-racial structures that are predatory on the economy in ways that organise work and social life towards valorising and mystifying phenotype. Skill, expertise, status have little to do with learning sans phenotype; even where these occur in the racial Other, their legitimacy is limited by institutional and other socio-cultural constraints that enforce the White norm and necessitate its manifestation through the widest array of socio-economic activities.

Works referred to
1. Graff, J. Harvey. 2010. *The literacy myth: literacy, education and demography*, Vienna Yearbook of Population Research, 2010, Vol. 8, Education and demography, Australian Academy of Sciences Press.
2. Collins, Randall. 2019. *The credential society: An historical sociology of education and stratification* Columbia University Press.

6

Diversity and the Politics of Data

Despite the issues we've discussed so far, the problem of diversity in the workforce and within sectors remains. Could this diversity be an indication of a changing society, a tendency towards equal opportunity, based on skills and credentials, or a tendency indicating the waning significance of phenotype in the job market and in society? Or could it be a carefully curated diversity? Large numbers of non-White immigrants work in sectors like health, real estate, and finance. Recall the research cited earlier indicating that supply and demand in the labour market determined the presence of immigrants in professional occupations and other sectors. This research showed that skilled immigrants from India, for example, were clustered in occupations that were oversupplied in Australia. We also cited research showing that supply and demand did not have a significant impact on the labour force outcomes of immigrants from the main English-speaking countries, and these immigrants were able to find jobs that matched their education and skills. In thinking of diversity in the workforce we must now consider the main source of information regarding immigrant occupations and income in Australia.

Most research and writing about immigration and the labour market rely on data produced by the Australian Bureau of Statistics (ABS). The ABS data on immigration or other social trends and indices informs and powerfully influences ideas about immigration, multiculturalism, and the labour market in Australia. It is commonly held that the ABS is not subject to political or other influences, and its job is simply the enumeration of social facts and trends. What this presumably means is that the ABS is not controlled by political parties; political influence is seen as something exerted by parties through bureaucratic institutions and other apparatus of governmental rule. The influence of culture, national ethos and national projects, and ethno-racial norms are seen as outside the scope of politics viewed as the domain of electoral battles and the social issues that come into this arena. The political is something that is determined by the party system, according to this view. We mentioned at the outset that the socio-racial determines everything in Australia. We also mentioned the importance of immigration and multiculturalism and how these have shaped all aspects of Australian life. The importance of cultural pluralism to the self-image of a nation built on immigration cannot be underestimated. The success of this pluralism depends on the integration of immigrants into Australian society.

An important aspect of integration is the ability of immigrants to find work that helps them build life in a new land, and, in the process, contribute to the host society. In recent decades,

Australia has built its immigration program on skilled migration. Unlike the post-WWII waves of immigration, the current flows of immigration are characterised by skilled migrants capable of working in professional or similar roles in the host economy. The category "professional" includes a wide variety of jobs that involve "analytical, conceptual and creative tasks through the application of theoretical knowledge and experience in the fields of the arts, media, business, design, engineering, the physical and life sciences, transport, education, health, information and communication technology, the law, social sciences and social welfare (ANZSCO)". Going by this definition, the ABS surveys show that most skilled migrants report an income from a professional occupation. ABS figures, for example, show that skilled migrants have good labour force outcomes, and their earnings are better than incumbent workers. According to the ABS, the number of skilled immigrants reporting professional occupations is proportionally higher than the local population reporting professional jobs.

We must remember that the ABS relies on self-enumeration when it comes to professions. Immigrants as professionals and managers, for instance, outnumber labourers, cooks, drivers, care worker, retail clerks, etc[1]. The question arises as to where these immigrants are in the workforce? Also, when we add up labourers, drivers, machinery operators, care workers, and retail staff, the numbers are higher than those who report a professional occupation. Regarding the professionally-employed immigrants: are they in the private sector or are they in the public sector? If so, how do we determine if the roles they are in use their education or are commensurate with their professional background? The ABS says that for the year 2016-2017 migrant taxpayers generated $112 billion in total personal income. About 91 per cent of total income was employee income ($102 billion); over half (61 per cent) migrant taxpayers held a skilled visa and skilled migrants generated 72 per cent of the total income earned by migrants.[2] For those who report an occupation not related to their qualification, the proportion of immigrants over incumbents is marginally higher. The reasons given by Australians and immigrants for not being in an occupation related to their qualifications include lack of interest or being happy in their current job.[3]

The picture presented by these statistical snapshots have little to say about the labour market dynamics that we've discussed so far. Why is this the case? If the problem of skill mismatch or the difficulties migrants face in finding suitable employment (which is to say that they are welcomed as drivers, cooks, security guards, entry- to mid-level office workers, and care workers, i.e., "immigrant jobs") is reflected in the statistical picture painted by the ABS, would the picture of a liberal, plural, migrant destination faced with skill shortages in the expanding economy hold? And if the reasons for this skill mismatch were not just a matter of supply and demand or lack of cultural fit, but included the blockages created by the White norm, and the needs of distributing economically productive people in low-skilled sectors of the economy, could we keep our faith in the idea of a race-neutral economy faced with skills shortages and the inclusive democracy that is built on such an economy? Surely, the ABS couldn't afford to challenge the nationalistic self-image of an immigrant nation. If the figures point to the social necessity of pushing non-White people into certain sectors of the job market, the census ceases to maintain its relevance and function, like all the other institutions of Australia, in promoting ideals that preserve and enable racial hegemony. This is to say that the census data add to the myths of a harmonious pluralising society moving towards a post-racial paradise.

The place of the immigrant in Australia, the place of the immigrant in the labour market, in the housing market, in the school system, is the place accorded to non-White races in White Australia. This overriding social compulsion goes beyond the rhetoric of multiculturalism; it uses multiculturalism and mass immigration to further its own needs for socio-political hegemony. This is the socio-racial as manifested in the ABS data and the social science research guided by the ABS.

In Shades of Citizenship — Race and the Census in Modern politics Melissa Nobles says that "politics infuses census-taking". Census bureaus do not operate in a vacuum, nor do they stand above or apart from society. Instead, the wider economic, political and cultural forces profoundly shape the nature of the categories and the data they generate. Analysing the "mutually reinforcing dynamic between concepts of race, censuses and citizenship", Nobles says: "census bureaus are not politically neutral institutions, employing impartial methods, but state agencies that use census methods and data as instruments of governance". Nobles writes that race is not an objective category to be counted, but a "fluid and internally contradictory discourse, partly created by and embedded in institutional processes, including those of the census itself". Nobles argues that racial discourses influence "both the rationales for public policy and its outcomes.... Public policies not only use racial census data; these data assist in the development of public policy." Importantly, Nobles writes, individuals and groups seek to alter the terms of racial discourse to advance political and social aims, and to this end censuses are targeted by socio-political groups with a view to further political goals. According to Nobles, while there's little debate on the significance of race in contemporary society, there is little understanding of how race works in society. Nobles is one among many noted scholars who emphasise the role of the census in racial discourses in society. Nobles writes that "census bureaus are typically overlooked as participants in the creation and perpetuation of race".

Nobles argues that a discussion of citizenship and race would seem a far remove from census-taking, but censuses register and reinforce racial identifications germane to citizenship through categorisation itself. Census-taking is political in origin and with consequences "competes with concerted efforts by international bodies and national governments to ensure and demonstrate its political impartiality". The role of the census in shaping racial politics has been underestimated and under-studied by social scientists. Census bureaus as state institutions determining the benefits and penalties of racial memberships through the categories created to collect data have been understudied so far. The role the census plays and the importance of the census categories in Australia have failed to gain any serious study so far. Ethnic and racial categories are taken to be natural or given; yet these categories, like in other ethnically diverse societies, are constantly being renegotiated as the demographics of a society changes, and, as existing norms are contested, adapted, and appropriated, in and through censuses and the politics of diversity and multiculturalism. This same insight applies in significant ways to the processes of self-enumeration that generate labour force and income statistics related to race/ethnicity and immigration in Australia.

Let us keep these insights in mind while thinking of the ABS and its data about immigrants. Given the challenges immigrants face in Australia, economically and culturally, could we say that the ABS plays a part in creating a picture of a racially inclusive and harmonious society, a picture that is at odds with the labour market dynamics we've discussed? Wouldn't this picture, then, be part of an attempt to reinforce the idea of an immigrant nation built upon successive waves of migration from all corners of the world creating a racially diverse contemporary society? If diversity means increasing numbers of people from a variety of cultures and races, then Australia has diversity. However, this diversity has done little to modify the trends of labour market segmentation by race. We started off with the question about who speaks for migration and the immigrant in Australia. The most authoritative and legitimised voices are those of White Australia speaking for the non-White races down under.

Colic-Peisker writes that the official recognition of qualifications in Australia reflects the logic of cultural proximity. Official recognition of qualifications may be necessary for public sector jobs, but it is neither necessary nor sufficient in the private sector. Employers are those who pass the ultimate judgement on the value of a person's skills through employing them.

The class nature of Australian society and how class shapes

outcomes related to work, the arts, and the professions has been written about. The class nature of the occupational structure, the division of labour, and the distribution of personnel in the labour market in almost every nation has been researched and written about extensively. In Australia, the school system is known to be skewed in favour of privileged sections of society in terms of the resources schools have, the academic outcomes of private versus public schools, the ethnic make-up of selective schools and public schools, and how schooling is a pathway to upward mobility; a great deal of literature has also documented the social composition of professional groups in society and the socio-economic backgrounds, i.e., the privileged backgrounds, of professionals. Schools and school catchment areas in immigrant gateway cities are sites around which racial segregation in schools and in residential areas are organised. We discuss this in the sections on settlement patterns in Sydney. All these trends show that work and the occupations are matters of choice for those who have the privilege to choose and reserve these choices to members of their own groups through mechanisms of social closure. It is important to bear in mind, and it cannot be overemphasised, that such choices are not made in a social vacuum. The nature of schooling, higher education, housing, and the labour market all work together to promote the value of race and racial hegemony in society.

The myths about work and an analogy with the creative arts

Just like social scientists refer to work as if it is race-neutral and post-racial, common ideas and discourses of art see it as above the mundane and unpleasant realities of racism. Recall that we mentioned earlier that work and its rewards are highly racialised in Australia, and so are the arts and culture and all forms of creative expression. Yet the idea of the artist and cultural expression shares much in common with our ideas of work. When we think of art or writing we focus on the individual elements related to the production of a piece of writing, or work of art. Its social aspects are held in the background to emphasise the individual elements of productivity and creation. Contemporary culture promotes the idea that art is above or apart from society, that art holds a mirror to society, or it challenges social beliefs and promotes new ways of thinking. This idea of art as a disinterested form of activity, in the sense that it is not embedded in social conflicts that shape society, or at least not all social conflicts, has been critiqued extensively for a long time now.

Yet ideas about art and artists still rely on or hymn the artist as a creative truth teller, a sensitive individual, solitary, and so on. The racial nature of all White art, all art, its role in promoting White or ethno-racial ideas of beauty, truth, and sociality is well known, yet we still see the writer, musician, painter as an individual who shows us society in a new light when White art rarely does that, or rather it promotes the White norm as universal. This is to say that art sanctifies social life and responds to the call or needs of ethno-racial communities that seek imaginary social spaces and themes. The same holds for work and the professions too. Our ideas about work, the work ethic, work being integratory or able to transcend the conflicts and divides in society are like the mystical ideas we have about art.

Racism and opportunity hoarding in the labour market

We think of intellectuals or journalists as people committed to their profession or art despite their social moorings. We rarely acknowledge that work, the professions, like art, is extremely racialised. We think a mechanic or builder is just focused on their trade, but we do not think enough about the social necessities that manifest themselves in a builder's projects, or a mechanic's workshop. In private life we rarely make calculations and choices regarding tradies or doctors or teachers or accountants that are race-neutral. This is not to say that a technician's race is more important than their skills, but often we find service providers organised and segmented in ways that tap into racialised markets and audiences. The racialised nature of work means that the paths to occupations and the rewards like the legitimacy and status that come with an occupation are fundamentally racialised phenomena. This racialised nature of work and its rewards explain the blockages non-White races face; researchers in the United States also term this as "opportunity hoarding".

The racially segmented Australian workforce is a site that thrives on opportunity hoarding. Usually, this is seen as a White versus non-White race problem. However, the segmentation of the labour market means that opportunities are hoarded in all ethnic niches and enclaves, like the retail trades, manufacturing, construction, health care, the law, teaching etc. The discourses of efficiency, the sentiments around common everyday slogans like "Aussie jobs for Australians" all sanctify this widespread phenomenon of opportunity hoarding in Australia. It is mistaken to see this as aberration or arising from prejudice when it is systemic and widespread, a well-entrenched social phenomenon. The racialised, segmented workforce in Australia works with the education and training system, ensuring the right people are in the right places as determined by the racial caste system. Just as we have come to accept class as important in determining an individual's life chances, it is important to make every attempt to see how race, ethno-culture, and pigment shape opportunities, and structure the labour market in Australia.

This is also why so-called minorities write and speak about the cognitive dissonance they face while working in professions or organisations where their pigment/race makes them hyper-visible and seemingly out-of-place. The presence of racial minorities in organisations that are organised to promote White work and White norms is seen from the perspective of diversity as a sign of progress, as an index of a diversifying workforce. When work and race are inextricably bound together it is hard to see how White spaces can transform themselves towards a plural or post-racial world of work and social life.

Let us stay with the analogy of art and writing: We are habituated to think that books or works of art are authored by individuals, since this is the idea culture promotes. When we look at the nature of writing in Australia, the literary landscape and the themes that continue to animate it and keep the literary assembly line in motion, it is difficult not to see scholars, authors, writers as individuals distributed by the literary intellectual system in the right place to be associated with writings and books that have already been written in some form or the other. The author-function works through phenotype in promoting the idea of creativity and individuality. Precisely this is the situation with the job market too. Once we stop thinking of the labour market as an institution peopled by individual job seekers who seek to fulfil their talents and aspirations, it becomes clear that Australia's White institutions, the courts, the media, the police, the universities, political parties, activist networks and so on need White personnel in keeping with the White norm that is actualised through the racial formation that is Australia. The racial-caste system in Australia shapes the nature of credentialling through the institutions of education and the labour market working together to promote White hegemony. Ideas of talent, aptitude, class, culture, sexuality, diversity, and gender make the presence of whiteness in all spheres of Australian life look like a matter of individual choice when the racialised social situation necessitates the promotion of ethno-racial hegemony through these realms of social life. This system of White occupations necessitates the exclusion of non-Whites based on discourses that entrench the hold of whiteness on the social imaginaire.

Immigration scholarship, labour market economists, sociologists and race scholars in Australia confine the discussion of jobs and upward mobility to a matter of discrimination. Writing about discrimination and the institutional imperatives that shape racism in Brazil, Sociologist Edward E. Telles says, in Race in another America:

"Institutions often discriminate, regardless of the beliefs held by those who work in them. Institutional pressures to maintain a racial hierarchy often structure individual choices. Attorney Hedio Silva, the director of unions, provides an example of how individuals may act in discriminatory ways even though not of a racist mind themselves. He describes the example of a white personnel director who does not hold antiblack sentiments, who feels comfortable around blacks, socializes with them, and perhaps is married to a black woman, but is under institutional pressure to justly keep black workers, including members of his own family, from formal employment; he also knows that if he hires black workers, he puts his own job in jeopardy. Although the firm has not explicitly told him to admit only white workers, he knows that he will be evaluated on his ability to hire workers who maintain or improve the institutional profile of his company. Given a nationally shared ideal of what constitutes a desirable profile, he surmises that white workers are preferable. The general culture disseminates and accepts the idea of a racial hierarchy, which Brazilians in turn perceive as natural; this provides them with a logic for understanding and legitimizing the racial order."

This nationally-shared ideal of what constitutes a desirable profile for an organisation in Australia, and what constitutes a desirable profile for Australia as a nation, are crucial factors in determining the function of the labour market. There is no dearth of concern on the matter of discrimination in the labour market, and the institutionalised responses to it advocating multiculturalism and diversity.

That the labour market is a crucial institution of a racial formation can be seen when we look at the labour market outcomes of immigrants from the Global South compared to those from Europe. For Australia to maintain its image as a White society, both to itself and to global society, the function of the labour market in distributing races to occupations and segments of the labour market is crucial. This trend is in keeping with Australia's colonial past. As mentioned earlier, to understand the workings of race in and through the labour market, we must consider the function of temporary immigration in the Australian labour market. We turn to this in the next chapter. Through this discussion we attempt to show that phenotype/race structures the labour market across the categories citizen/non-citizen, permanent resident/temporary migrant used by researchers to show that the formal rights given to immigrants who attain residency/citizenship spare them from the harsher realities of race and the racisms of the labour market.

Works referred to

1. https://www.abs.gov.au/statistics/people/people-and-communities/perspectives-migrants/2018-19-financial-year#employment-and-non-school-qualifications-by-visa-stream accessed 27.2.22.
2. https://www.abs.gov.au/statistics/people/people-and-communities/personal-income-migrants-australia/latest-release.
3. https://www.abs.gov.au/statistics/people/people-and-communities/perspectives-migrants/2018-19-financial-year#employment-and-non-school-qualifications-by-visa-stream.
4. Nobles, Melissa. 2000. *Shades of Citizenship — Race and the Census in Modern politics.* Stanford University Press.
5. Telles, Edward E. *Race in another America: The significance of skin color in Brazil.* 2014. Princeton University Press.
6. Colic-Peisker, Val. 2011. *Employment success of skilled and professional NESB migrants: the most important measures of Australian multiculturalism* Joint Standing Committee on Migration.

7

Temporary Migration and the White saviours

Permanent migration is no longer the only driver of Australia's record population growth. In the last two decades the number of temporary migrants in Australia more than doubled to nearly 900,000. In the first decade of the 2000s there were about 350,000 international students, working holiday makers, and temporary skilled workers in Australia. These three categories of temporary migration increased the population by 40,000 people a year on average, says the Scanlon Foundation's report on temporary migration. The number of permanent migrants is capped, while there is no ceiling on temporary migration. Emphasising the transformation to Australia's migration regime, the report says that in 2018 there were more than 2.2 million people in the country on temporary visas. In that same year, Australia accepted about 190,000 permanent migrants.

The break-up of the groups comprising temporary migrants is crucial to our argument. For the period we are discussing here, the largest group of temporary migrants are international students (575,000). This was followed by skilled work visas (152,000), and working holiday makers (136,000). Excluding short-stay visitors (they spend less than a year in the country) and New Zealanders (682,000), there were one million temporary migrants with the right to work in Australia in 2018. Most of these temporary migrants came from the Asian region, notably India and China. Many sectors of the Australian economy, like aged care, hospitality, education, construction, and horticulture, have come to rely on these migrants. As is well known now, international students are the backbone of the country's largest export industry, education. In 2018, this industry employed 130,000 people and was worth $28.6 billion a year. In terms of its weight in the economy, the higher education sector's contribution, backed by international student enrolments, rivals the importance of Australia's auto-manufacturing sector in its heyday.

While COVID led to a dramatic fall in these figures, the post-COVID years have registered impressive numbers. Media reports say that 40 per cent of international student spending is on tuition fees and the rest on consumption of goods and services in Australia. In 2023, spending by international students accounted for more than half of Australia's economic growth, according to a report in the *AFR*.

Discussing international students from India, and the transformation of skilled Indian migration to Australia, Lesleyanne Hawthorne writes that from 1999, when international students were eligible to migrate to Australia, there was a dramatic surge in the number of international students from India, and their numbers increased tenfold over the next decade. In that first decade, up to 70 per cent of Indian students ended up gaining residency in Australia. From 2005, Indian students started aligning their course choices with Australia's skilled occupation demand list. According to Hawthorne, while the choice of course enabled Indian students gain residency in Australia, it constrained their access to early employment as the courses were in fields already oversupplied in Australia. Analysis of migrant employment outcomes showed Indian students (less than half of them had fulltime jobs) struggled to get fulltime employment. Employers, reportedly, felt deluged by applications from international students. However, although Indian students struggled to find entry-level work in the fields they were qualified in, they had high labour force participation rates. According to Hawthorne, labour market demand for skills was the critical factor determining the success or failure of international students in gaining employment aligned to their field of study.

Hawthorne says that international students today represent an elastic and rapidly growing resource, "an adjunct workforce in waiting". They have the potential to offer host country governments and employers a "productivity premium". They are far younger than mature migrants selected offshore, and they are "self-funded to meet domestic workforce demand". Studies showed that while they had high labour force participation rates, their earnings were substantially lower than migrants selected offshore.

So: international students from the Global South are sought after in Australia as valuable consumers of Australian education; they are also important players in Australia's low-wage casualised work sectors. The Australian Bureau of Statistics (ABS) figures estimate that more than 50 per cent of international students undertake paid employment. The research cited above on international students and the labour market shows that most students from China, Malaysia, India, Nepal etc are not able to find jobs that match or use their educational qualifications. We should pause and ask if race plays a role in determining their place in the labour force? Researchers attribute the labour market outcomes to supply and demand factors, or cultural attributes. These explanations are valid, but supply and demand are not just phenomena that can be restricted to neutral economic factors, whatever that may mean. It is as though race does not structure the labour market. If one relies on an "economics" above or free of race, culture, ethnicity, colour, or gender, supply and demand would be a mechanical process; economics would be above and beyond socio-cultural or ethno-racial necessities. The "invisible hand" would be behind supply, demand, distribution, pricing, and wages.

Can we assume that the "invisible hand" structuring Australia's labour market is so invisible? Or should we think the norms of ethno-race, that ethno-culture determines the distribution of workers to roles in society? Couldn't we legitimately see this as the workings of a caste order? The labour market does not just distribute people by race to occupations. It also determines their status in society through the returns the nature of their jobs get students and temporary migrants. All of this is usually explained as economic phenomena, as if race did not overdetermine these trends in society.

While the role of race is implied or acknowledged in academic analyses on immigration and the labour market, there is also a persistent attempt to organise analyses on the principles of formal equality and rights that minimise or eliminate the role of phenotype in determining one's status in society. As mentioned earlier, these are examples of neutrality and colourblindness that structure Australian analyses of race relations today. Let us go on to look at the labour market stories of temporary migrants.

The most widely-publicised concerns relating to temporary migrants are related to their difficulties in the labour market, and the systemic nature of the abuses and exploitation they face. As mentioned at the outset, the category "temporary migrant" is made up of international students, working holiday makers, and skilled employer-sponsored migrants, besides tourists and working holiday makers. The abuse of temporary migrants in the workplace is seen as detrimental to the rights and interests not just of guest workers but also domestic labour that could potentially be employed in sectors known to be reliant on immigrant labour. The systemic nature of the exploitation of temporary migrants is seen to be a violation of Australia's fair work culture, labour market laws, and standards. The discussion, while it cannot conceal the fact that immigrants from the Global South are the main victims, builds up a regulatory and rights-based case for formal equality.

As stated previously, Australia's work practices and culture have been shaped historically by ideas of race and the racial caste system. We stated earlier that society in many ways is a euphemism for race, a socio-political project for racial aggrandisement and hegemony; multiculturalism is the latest phase in this history of White supremacy.

Writing about the regulatory challenges involved in temporary migration, Joanna Howe and Rosemary Owens say: "A basic question to ask might be whether this 'new' global phenomenon is really new at all. In many ways, temporary labour migration today echoes colonial indentured labour and older forms of guest work, for example, Chinese labour in Malaya and the Dutch East Indies, and Indian 'coolies' in the West Indies". Notice how, for Australian scholars, the examples of temporary labour migration are not usually associated with settler colonial societies; the racial nature of work in Australia, practices like blackbirding, for example, are not relevant to contemporary agricultural workforce issues today; this is to say that the exploitation of temporary migrants today is not commonly viewed as a continuation of Australia's history of race relations and the organisation of work and life based on this. As mentioned earlier, the racial nature of this phenomenon is seen to be unrelated to the history of Australia.

Citing factors identified by the UN Special Rapporteur on the human rights of migrants in the report to the UN Human Rights Council, Howe writes that the concentration of global capital has led to demand for both highly skilled workers and low-skilled workers. Temporary migrants are concentrated in jobs that locals will not do and in sectors where exploitation is more likely due to cost pressures and the competitiveness of these sectors. Howe writes about the tendency of "regulation in the global era to privilege the interests of capital". This framing of the problem is an example of the silences about the ethno-racial nature of capital, the unwillingness or blindness towards the historical facts about capital as always already racialised.

This silence about the fundamentally racial nature of capital then becomes a way for an army of Australian White saviours to go out exposing offending businesses and, in the process, sanctifying Australia's fair work culture (where the meaning of fair is both just and White). The systemic nature of these abuses is located in a race-neutral capitalist economy in need of low wage labour to maintain its profits and provide local markets with cost-effective products, produce, and services. This is not to say that the issue is simply a matter of White versus non-White; however, the widespread exploitation of migrant workers in Australia is framed as an economic and legal matter that can be redressed within White Australia's fair legal and social system, even when commentators point out the systemic nature of the abuses and trace these back to capital or neo-liberalism and its dual and/or segmented labour markets that facilitate the abuse of worker rights. As mentioned, this is an example of a predicament that cannot be named or discussed explicitly in Australia: the manner of inclusion of non-Whites in a White society.

Howe says: *"The dominant regulatory approach of receiving states has been to facilitate temporary labour flows according to an economic rationale. [...] However, the economic rationale serves the interests of global business particularly well, because it creates a larger and more flexible labour market from which to select workers. Temporary labour migration generally means the entry into the local labour market of workers from countries with less protective or developed regulation. In competing with local workers, these migrant workers are usually willing to accept lower wages and worse conditions because their frame of reference is their country of origin. Further, they usually form a more compliant workforce because of their twin desire to recoup the costs of their investment in the migratory process and to send remittances home. They are especially motivated to be compliant when there is the possibility of securing permanent residency."*

As valuable and instructive as such analyses may be, we must ask a question that is not included here: do temporary migrants like international students, or migrants working in agriculture, have a choice in the work they do? Migration scholars and other observers believe that if temporary migrants have better rights in the labour market they could evade exploitative employment conditions. Howe says that although it is conventionally assumed that the migrant worker is the subject of law regulating temporary labour migration, a common strand in the regulatory approach of receiving countries is to develop policies and laws around temporary migration that favour global capital.

Temporary migrants are concentrated in metropolitan areas and mostly work in sectors like hospitality, food, and accommodation. They are also a crucial part of Australia's agricultural workforce that relies on the availability of temporary migrants for seasonal work. The cost of labour is said to be important in ensuring profits and commercial viability for businesses relying on temporary migrants. In sectors like cleaning in metropolitan CBDs, according to the Cleaning Accountability Framework (CAF), international students make up as much as 85 per cent of the workforce. Let us look at other examples of writing on this matter.

Although the problem is global and has local particularities in all the immigrant destinations, let us look at an official Australian government document discussing this problem. *The Report of the Migrant Workers' Taskforce* (2019) discussing the problem of "wage theft" says that wage exploitation is not just unfair to migrant workers, but it undermines Australia's labour market by undercutting local jobseekers and employers who want to play the game by the rules. The exploitation of migrant workers affects Australia's reputation for fairness in economic and social relationships. The report sees migrant worker exploitation as a complex arena where employment, migration, corporation, taxation, and other laws intersect. As an example, it cites labour hire companies underpaying overseas workers that may also be avoiding tax obligations, and be involved in sham contracting or phoenixing to avoid employee entitlements. The report sees the problem as one driven largely by rogue employers operating in the Australian labour market.

Citing the reasons for the exploitation of migrant workers, the report lists consumer demand for low priced products, competitive pressures, an abundant supply of temporary migrants, and a culture of underpayment in some sectors of the economy. The report sees Australia's legislative framework adequate to protect all types of workers, locals, or temporary migrants.

We must ask now: How can the law treat a temporary migrant, a worker from the Global South, on the same terms as a local White worker? Despite the rituals of the legal system and the appearances of neutrality, objectivity, rationality, and the concern for impartiality termed "fairness", couldn't we stop to ask if this term "fairness" is meant literally, that is: innocence or indifference to the whiteness of the legal system and its ethnocentric ideas of legality and impartiality? Isn't this formal equality a strong form of race neutrality, behind which and through which (i.e., through this White Australian national legislative framework) a labour migration regime is facilitated, bringing into the country non-White workers to serve a White society and economy in a subservient position? Then using the plight of this non-White workforce for the aggrandisement of White law and its ideas of equality? Isn't this theatre, this public spectacle, a means towards the aggrandisement of White Australia? Couldn't this be the reason why the investigations and campaigns against the exploitation of temporary migrants have mostly been a form of action against the informal labour market in Australia that services Australia's formal White labour market? Little wonder that this concern about the reputation of Australia's fair system has mostly resulted in targeting ethnic businesses and employers and in the process created a scapegoat. The rogue employer, the people smuggler, the dodgy ethnic entrepreneur making profit through stealing wages, and so on and so forth. No doubt, the informal labour market is rife with all types of exploitations of migrants, but can we say that the local White community is not complicit in this, directly and indirectly? Can we dissociate these practices of exploitation from White ideas on third world societies and cultures, and White customs of leisure and recreation in the third world as spaces of pleasure made easily affordable to Western Whiteness? Is the plight of the third world migrant in Australia not connected to White ideas about non-White societies and peoples in relation to whiteness? As we mentioned previously, race neutrality derives from and thrives on this compartmentalisation of social problems.

Writing about labour protection for temporary migrants,

Joo-Cheong Tham, Iain Campbell and Martina Boese discuss two local examples of exploitation of temporary migrant workers: workers on temporary visas (457 visa workers) and international student workers. They discuss employer non-compliance with protective workplace regulations and attribute this non-compliance to the interaction of the vulnerability of temporary migrant workers with employment practices in poorly-regulated industries. The researchers stress the structural nature of non-compliance in industries where temporary workers are concentrated, and refute the idea that these practices occur because of dishonest employers or individuals. Discussing the principal dedicated temporary labour migration program (457 visas) in Australia at the time of writing, the authors say: *"a major review of data collected by the workplace enforcement agencies has concluded that 'achieving widespread employer standards in Australia is a major and ongoing challenge' and non-compliance by employers is 'likely to have increased in the wake of labour market deregulation and the decline of trade union strength'"*. The authors say that non-compliance is particularly acute in relation to temporary migrant workers: in 2012, in response to growing complaints of abuse from migrant workers, the Fair Work Ombudsman (FWO) established an Overseas Worker Team, and in the following year complaints from these workers accounted for 10 per cent of all complaints received by the FWO, an increase of 25 per cent from the previous year. For this period, the authors say, a third of all legal actions initiated by the FWO involved migrant workers.

The authors then say that the evidence on non-compliance

in relation to 457 visa holders is conflicting, with some studies saying reported violations of their rights were not more than five per cent of workers included in a Department of Immigration survey of 4,000 457 visa workers. However, the researchers say, figures from the FWO suggest a more significant problem of non-compliance. In 2013-14 the FWO assessed 1,029 entities and 1,902 primary visa holders. More than 20 per cent of these entities were referred to the Immigration Department due to concerns relating to wages and the visa holders not working in nominated occupations. The authors cite the Australian Council of Trade Unions (ACTU)'s submission to a 2015 Senate Inquiry into temporary work visas: the ACTU "compiled a list of cases involving non-compliance in relation to 457 visa workers, arguing that these cases point to a pattern of abuse".

Interestingly, the authors say: *"It should be remembered that not all discrimination against 457 visa workers is illegal, and whether it is depends very much on the reason for the discrimination. That noted, the 2012 Immigration Department survey indicates that overt discrimination in the workplace against 457 visa workers only affects a minority of workers. Whilst 16 per cent of the survey's respondents stated that they had been discriminated against based on skin colour, ethnic origin and/or religious beliefs in the past 12 months, only 0.5 per cent indicated that such discrimination occurred in the workplace"*. The writers say that even if only a minority are affected by discrimination, the consequences are serious for these workers and they include gross underpayment among other practices of unfair treatment.

So, we have a situation where workers of colour are in sectors and jobs that are not White in the sense that few White workers work in these jobs. The feelings of temporary migrants of being marginalised or treated differently do not count as discrimination, as many of them work in nominated occupations and are paid an agreed-upon wage. We see here an example of the limitations and the narrow ideas of discrimination and the workplace.

While the larger social situation and the labour market that arises from this social scenario facilitates the conditions of placement of people of colour in certain types of work in a segmented labour market, the law on discrimination is silent on this larger scenario of White and non-White work. This is to say that the racialised nature of work is beyond the concern of the law. The just-cited research attributes the vulnerability of temporary migrant workers to workplace relationships prevalent in what they call "hazardous" industries. We will come back to this dichotomy in the labour market that migration researchers use to analyse the problems migrant workers face. We must pause to reflect here if this dual labour market is not related to the ethno-racial facts of Australian social life.

Tham, Campbell, and Boese name hospitality, childcare, agriculture, construction, and cleaning as examples of hazardous industries relying on temporary migrant workers. *"The divergence between well-regulated and poorly regulated industries provides a platform for industry or sectoral patterns of non-compliance. Not only are standards lower in the poorly regulated industries, but they also tend to be those industries with high levels of employer non-compliance."* The top five industries temporary skilled 457 visa holders were concentrated (according to statistics from March 2015) were

1. accommodation and food services, 2. construction, 3. other services, 4. health care and social assistance, and 5. Information media and telecommunications.

According to Tham, Campbell, and Boese, studies showed that the experiences of 457 visa holders varied dramatically by industry: those working in health care had few concerns, and these workers were well integrated with little evidence of employer non-compliance. They attribute such outcomes to better regulation and high union membership. In other words, being part of the Australian workforce with all its benefits resulted in fewer complaints from temporary migrants.

So, sectors with White workers have better protections and rewards. Also, it is implied here that the regular workforce does not treat workers differently on grounds of race or country of origin. We must go back to this point later.

Tham, Campbell, and Boese then say that in several industries non-compliance is *"clearly more of a problem for 457 workers. It is noteworthy that the three main industry divisions in which 457 visa holders are employed are also 'hazardous' industries known for high level of non-compliance for all workers. As a result, 457 visa holders have been caught up in practices prevalent within these industries."*

In relation to international students, the authors say: *"employer non-compliance is widespread in connection with international students. International students are more concentrated than 457 visa holders and the industries in which they are concentrated, such as accommodation and food services, cleaning and retail, are precisely those that are identified as poorly regulated and 'hazardous' industries."*

It should be kept in mind that, in arguing for the role of race and the silence about the centrality of race in Australia's migration program, it is not implied that these analyses are flawed or that they do not raise important issues. However, they do keep the problem of race in the margins if they raise it at all. Our argument here is for the overdetermining role of race in all social phenomena in Australia. This should not be seen as a hierarchy of causes or factors leading to the marginalisation of sections of workers in Australia. However, seeing race as an epiphenomenon or the result of economic factors ends up minimising the racialised nature of social life and work in Australia.

Let us quickly go over another example. Peter Mares, in his book *Not Quite Australian*, argues for better protections and rights for temporary migrants, including granting them citizenship after a certain period of stay in Australia, in recognition of the vital role they play in the labour force and as a permanent presence in contemporary Australia. Discussing the exploitation and abuses against temporary migrants, the book says that a long-term inquiry by the Fair Work Ombudsman revealed systemic and widespread abuses of migrant workers in Australia's agribusiness supply chains. The inquiry revealed that major players in the chicken processing industry routinely exploited working holiday makers. Other studies also found that there is systemic and widespread exploitation in the food, hospitality, and cleaning sectors employing mostly international students. The book says that job ads in the ethnic media violate Australia's laws against discrimination in that they specifically ask for the nationality, height, weight, or gender of workers, and offer below award wages.

While these findings tell us harsh truths about the informal economy and "ethnic enclaves", they also echo White Australia's ideas about "ethnic enclaves" and the culture of work in these businesses. Further, they show us the unquestioning faith White Australia has in its own customs, conventions, and laws on discrimination, on open inquiry, and so on. It shows us the innocence or indifference that White Australia has in understanding the nature and logic of the privileges that come with White hegemony and the standards of living and status this privilege (socio-political power) has ensured for select groups of people.

Speaking of the living conditions of temporary migrants, Mares says that apart from being underpaid and overworked many temporary migrant workers, including international students, are forced to live in overcrowded apartments. We must keep this point in mind when we discuss White homes and White spaces in the final chapters. Who gets to live in a decent home, and what is decent housing in Australia? Are these ideas race neutral? Are these spaces/homes not connected to sectors of the job market, just as the dirty, dangerous, and demeaning jobs are tied to poor housing conditions? Can we see these two sides of Australia as unrelated? Or is there a social process that produces and co-constitutes this phenomenon of privilege and marginality, in a manner that has a history, a history that has produced White Australia and now is reproducing itself in what we think is a new and different world? Couldn't we see the marginality of the temporary migrant as the marginality of the racial other? And this marginality produced by White Australia?

The politics of the immigration debate

The research we have discussed so far gives an indication of how the problems of immigration are framed in the public sphere. The labour market integration of immigrants is one of the most important concerns related to immigration in Australia. This should come as no surprise, although immigration itself is much more than just its "economic" dimensions. Most migration today is labour migration, economically productive people looking for opportunities in the most lucrative labour markets. However, today's immigration flows are a challenge to the deeply-held beliefs and myths about Australia and its social ethos of tolerance and cosmopolitanism. Our ideas of Australia have been shaped by the myths about a society built on successive waves of permanent settlers, a society with the ability to integrate diverse communities through work, since a rich land is a land of opportunities, and these opportunities are primarily economic in nature. It is well known in the history of immigration that new settlers have always faced nearly overwhelming odds in the host society, and these challenges, in some shape or form, have been related to work. This is why, in discussions on recent migrants and their troubles, we are constantly reminded of the migrations of the Irish, the Greeks, the Italians, and their stories of displacement and eventual happy outcomes in Australia. It is assumed that history will repeat itself, there are universal laws of finding one's way in a new country and so on. These ideas and mythologies of immigration that circulate in society promote a commonsense view about immigration, and in doing this they hide the realities of a vastly transformed society, economy, and global village creating unprecedented and unresolvable deadlocks in society.

The current discussion on immigration and the labour market looks at the labour market in isolation from the rest of society, as though it's an institution capable of bringing together various sections of Australian society to work towards common ends. Underlying these discussions is the belief that work transcends the divides of society, or that social divides are primarily a matter of culture or class. Further, the privileging of culture and class as the principal divides in society functions to minimise the role and function of race in producing and maintaining culture and class through the institutions of training, education, and the labour market. Race then, in this framing, could only be a matter of discrimination, an aberration.

As said in the first chapter, we tend to think of work as though it were a neutral site, and the organisation of work and its ends in contemporary society (for instance a construction site, a factory, a hospital, or office) are free of the conflicts and competitions that surround the "labour market". When racism rears its head as a problem in the labour market it is always discussed as a matter of discrimination. The function of this framing, this debate on the labour market and immigration in Australia, is then to silence discussion about race and its role in the labour market. If we look at how the debate acknowledges the presence of racism in the labour market it becomes apparent that it uses anecdotal evidence to substantiate its belief that racism is only an aberration and not the norm in Australia's segmented labour market/s. This silence then is a way to repress the presence and role of the Other in Australia, to reassure the nation that whiteness remains, and retains its power in Australia (recall the references to Australia's fair system, and the potential damage to this reputation) despite the radical demographic and concurrent social transformations immigration is ushering in. It would be a form of wilful blindness to be oblivious of the racial anxieties undergirding these debates. To argue that the abuse and exploitation of workers in the informal sector is not related to the systemic necessities of White hegemony and its role in structuring and segmenting the labour market is also, consciously and subconsciously, an attempt to denigrate the racial other through race-neutral analyses of the economy and work.

The writings on the plight of the immigrant from the Global South in Australia — as a consequence of informality in the labour market, or inability to find suitable work, or inadequate rights to access the labour market's better opportunities — should not be viewed in isolation from the other discourses on immigration. Both the crisis narratives and the success narratives should be seen as working together to promote the myth of the White utopia that is Australia. This is to say that allaying the fears stemming from the crisis narrative on immigration is the other discourse on the successful and well-assimilated immigrant, the immigrant communities making up modern multicultural Australia: this discourse is shot through with powerful symbols of meritocracy, tales of heroism built around individual initiative overcoming odds in a new land, pluralism and tolerance, skill and ability, the modern economy with an abundance of jobs and openings for the right people, and so on. Just like racism being a matter of individual aberration, migrant success or failure in some way or the other, then, is a reflection of personal merit or failings. The labour market challenges of immigrants are almost always explained as the outcome of economic laws, supply and demand, cultural fit, social skills, not having the rights to work in Australia as a result of coming into the country illegally, and so on. It is rarely acknowledged, except in the few writings on skill wastage, that legal and illegal immigrants often face similar challenges in Australia, and these challenges are not unrelated to ethnicity.

Labour market surveys and the population Census of Australia always speak of the high labour force participation rates of immigrants, and this is seen as a sign of a smoothly functioning society. Survey after survey confirms the widely-held social science dogma that immigrants — after a period of adjustment in the host society, which includes unemployment, and/or downward mobility — find suitable work eventually, and over the years are well adjusted members of the community.

In these writings and debates on immigrants and the labour market, some things are clear: labour migration dominates immigration into Australia, and the changes in the immigration regime in Australia in recent decades coincide with structural changes in the labour market manifesting as the move from agriculture and manufacturing to services, real estate, higher education, health care, the creative services etc. It is also apparent that the debate grapples with the problem of people from low-income countries with fewer jobs migrating for work to the most lucrative labour markets.

The general picture of Australia is one of a booming modern post-industrial economy, a computerised, digitised society awash with opportunities for people with the right skills to drive its cutting-edge knowledge economy. But this knowledge economy is also an ageing and affluent society generating high-wage and low-wage jobs. We are told that the high-wage jobs drive social and economic development, and the knowledge economy is leading us to a better tomorrow through research and development, and labour-saving technological innovation, all promoted and sustained by a healthy legal and political system. Our question here is limited to the issue of race: namely, how does race structure the knowledge economy? This is a topic in itself, and can easily generate countless books, and research. But if we stick to the numbers, the distribution of ethnicities by sectors in the labour market, it becomes hard to escape the conclusion that, when it comes to the better paying jobs with benefits, and the potential to build lucrative careers, we see White faces dominating these sectors. And around these jobs, servicing them and relying on their discretionary spending, are large numbers of non-White workers in food and hospitality, transport, facilities management etc. Diversity in the formal labour market and its "better" jobs gives the impression that skills and education are requisites, and immigrants from the Global South are mostly lacking in the right skills. Again, we are constantly told about the visa mix and residency status of immigrants. All of this serves to obfuscate the compulsions of race and its politics of structuring the labour market. This "function", so to speak, of the labour market is indispensable in maintaining White hegemony and the image of a White Australia.

The scholars and writers we've discussed are examples of White silences in the face of violence against the racial other, a violence organised in complex ways through the migration regime and its segmented labour market.

If education is required for jobs in the knowledge economy, we may ask, why are so many immigrants with formal qualifications and experience from the Global South unable to get jobs in sectors and industries that match their education? Why is it that immigrants from the UK or France are not seen in low wage sectors? Is it because all immigrants from the UK have the right qualifications for the best jobs? Is it because people from France, Germany, or Italy speak better English than immigrants from China, India, or Nigeria? Are all well-paying jobs in corporate Australia economically and socially necessary? Or do they reflect the social position/status and connections of those in highly paying jobs? If jobs are made to match one's status in the racial hierarchy, couldn't we think the labour market is subjected to the needs of wider processes of stratification and status? How else can we conceptualise the preponderance of White people in the most lucrative sectors? Are the jobs in these sectors, strictly speaking, productive? Or do they play a ceremonial role in ensuring the presence of whiteness and White people in lucrative sectors of the economy? In a time when higher education or the creative services are playing a vital role in Australia's economy, how can we explain the overwhelming whiteness of these industries? What is the symbolic function of the White educator or writer?

Surely there are issues of supply and demand that shape labour markets; for instance, education cannot possibly be geared towards producing the right number of skills as it is not possible to determine what the right number is, or what an industry's requirements may be at any point in the future; further, technology or demand can change the way an industry works, and so change the nature of occupations within an industry. This is all well known. But to insist that these factors outweigh the role of race is to ignore the function and prominence of race, and the necessity of the labour market in promoting racial welfare.

Through discussing the sectors of the labour market in isolation from one another, through analysing and categorising immigration as skilled or unskilled, we are forced to accept the terms of the debate and think that race does not overdetermine labour market outcomes. The presence of diversity within organisations, and the fact that across the different sectors and industries, considered overall, the labour market gives the impression of racial diversity as a social fact; however, this diversity hides the realities of race within organisations and sectors. The naked eye would have us believe that diversity is on the rise and it's a matter of education and individual ability, that times are changing, and so on. It is also the "racial commonsense" of the times that White people are in better jobs, and "minorities" as a group are not in the best jobs or careers. This is usually echoed in immigration scholarship: immigrants lack the cultural and social skills to function in some sectors of the labour market; or there are large numbers of immigrants lacking the required education coming in from poor countries, these immigrants find jobs in the low-wage sectors of the economy. Again, migration scholars say immigrants from the Global South come to the affluent world as locals in the rich north refuse to do dead-end demeaning jobs; that a rich economy and an affluent lifestyle create an economy around it. All this is applicable. However, unless we problematise the role of race in structuring the labour market we will remain blind to the distortions and misperceptions that social science promotes through its colourblind discourses.

In its 2020 migration outlook report, the OECD says that the presence of migrant workers in the labour markets of OECD countries has increased everywhere. In Australia, foreign-born workers have increased from 26 per cent to 30 per cent in the last 15 years. Sectors with the highest shares of workers in lower-skilled occupations are also the sectors with the highest share of migrant workers. In contrast, migrants are under-represented in public administration and in sectors with high shares of highly skilled employment. The share of migrants in domestic services has outgrown their share in any other sector in many OECD countries. If we include some sectors of health care as a type of domestic work, we might see a strikingly similar development in Australia. While the share of migrants has grown in service sectors, like domestic services, food, and aged care, the share of natives in these sectors has dropped dramatically. The OECD report says that, since 2005, sectoral disparities in the presence of migrants have grown. The share of migrants in the sectors, which already had a high share of migrants in 2005, has also grown disproportionately since, while the reverse was the case in sectors where migrants were under-represented. But migrants have also made inroads into finance, real estate, and information and communications.

Is this a contradictory picture, or is this how we should view the situation? Migrants are present in all sectors of the economy, even in sectors dominated by White people, and this shows that skill and education are crucial? Or could these social trends behind the distribution of migrants from the Global South in certain sectors be viewed as arising from labour market segmentation? Shouldn't we ask how the low wage and the high wage sectors are related, and if education plays a role in determining labour market outcomes for migrants? If so, how should we explain this role? Does the data say that immigrants land in the low-wage sectors due to insufficient skills and education? Or should we think that a contradictory picture is bound to be representative of a changing social situation characterised by racial diversity? If this is the case, does the data say that all White immigrants from the UK or France, in senior or suitably qualified roles, are educated and have the right qualifications and experience?

What could all this mean for the nature of work in the contemporary rich world? Could we, looking at the sectoral composition of the labour markets, retain our faith in participatory democracy? The historical ideas and discourses of the open egalitarian Western world and its tolerant and plural culture have a vice-like grip on public debate and official and unofficial ideas about society. Couldn't we ask if this image of society is the result of powerful political propaganda that hides the fact of ruthless social and political repression based on race and ethnicity? Isn't the nation-state a political project that enables and masks this project of racial domination?

Let us bring here again the points we made earlier about the widely-held belief among social scientists and others so inclined to think and speak of the economy as a neutral site; to discuss jobs and careers as means to an income. How can we make sense of the Australian economy if we keep status and prestige out of the equation? Can we not think the division of labour in everyday life is a racial division and does not correspond well with the textbook ideology and propaganda of the social scientists? How can we understand the role immigrants play in the economy and labour market if we keep whiteness and its beliefs in a racial hierarchy out of the equation? If we insist on a neutral economy, why is it that next to no White immigrants from the UK or the US are seen in the lowest-paid jobs in aged care? The value of whiteness determines the nature of the economy to a great extent in Australia, and this White nature of the economy determines the nature and the roles in the labour market. Surely, there are other important ways to see this phenomenon; for instance, people from low-income countries seeking work in better labour markets, or the prevalence of diversity, or the role of immigration in supplying sectors of the labour market that are facing shortages of workers.

We must look again at the occurrence and function of what is seen as discrimination in the labour market. The widespread nature of this phenomenon, its universal applicability in the job market and within organisations through making available the right opportunities and recognition to the right people, who often have the right attributes in relation to race and a racialised culture...is this all a random isolated occurrence? If it is not, couldn't we start thinking of this as a social phenomenon that is necessitated by the politics of race? An indispensable requirement in reproducing the whiteness of the professions, the racialisation of professional standards and culture, and through this the mystical belief in the superiority of whiteness in relation to efficiency, professionalism, and the centrality of whiteness to Australia? If the labour market was not controlled, if labour market outcomes were not overdetermined, how could the idea of a White Australia endure amidst all the changes in global society? When we argue that whiteness maintains a vice-like grip over the labour market, we must always remember that the labour market does not work in isolation from the politics of housing or urbanisation. Across these seemingly disparate social realms, whiteness exerts its political hold to reproduce our current ideas of work, and a desirable norm for social existence. This means that we have, in reality, not one but two or several Australias. The official White Australia, synonymous with democracy, liberalism, the politics of White egalitarianism, inclusion, and multiculturalism, and the other Australia living on the margins of this paradise, serving and servicing its needs, living in conditions that diverge from the White utopia — is this a random occurrence related to conditions of arrival or cultural circumstances? If so, how do people who have differing language abilities and cultural proclivities establish themselves and move up the economic ladder? How can we explain the coexistence of non-White immigrant marginality with the occurrence of upward mobility among non-Whites? Looking at the prevalence of socio-economic "marginality" among non-White immigrants, couldn't we say that marginality in a White society has been and continues to be tied to non-Whiteness? The function of social science, just like the function of popular culture in White Australia, then is to explain and sanitise the prevalence of precarity in work, poverty, lack of social protections, lesser rights, and marginalisation through paradigms promoting a race neutral economics. Is marginalisation the result of colourblind race neutral economic forces in Australia? Or is there reason to think that race overdetermines the social faultlines of contemporary Australia through the labour market, in the process producing and maintaining marginalisation in order to reproduce the whiteness of Australia and so the superiority of Western whiteness?

We must now turn to the politics of housing and the White home and White spaces in Australia.

Works referred to

1. *Off the scale but out of sight: The rise and rise of temporary migration* Scanlon Foundation Research Institute (narrative/02) (2018)
2. (https://www.afr.com/policy/economy/foreign-students-are-saving-the-economy-20240308-p5fasz).
3. https://www.cleaningaccountability.org.au/news/exploitation-of-international-students-in-australia/
4. Hawthorne, Lesleyanne, *The Recent Transformation of Indian Skilled Migration to Australia*, Aii Discussion Paper 1801, (2018)
5. Howe, Joanna, Rosemary, Owens *Temporary labour migration in the global era: the regulatory challenges*, Hart Publishing, (2016)
6. *A national disgrace: The Exploitation of Temporary Work Visa Holders Education and Employment References Committee* (2016)
7. *Report of the Migrant Workers' Taskforce* (2019), Commonwealth of Australia 2019
8. Joo-Cheong Tham, Iain Campbell and Martina Boese. 2016. "Why is Labour Protection for Temporary Migrant Workers so Fraught? A Perspective from Australia" in Howe, Joanna, Rosemary, Owens *Temporary labour migration in the global era: the regulatory challenges*, Hart Publishing.
9. Mares, Peter. 2016. *Not quite Australian*, Text Publishing.

10. OECD (2020), *International Migration Outlook* 2020, OECD Publishing, Paris, https://doi.org/10.1787/ec98f531-en

8

The Nostalgia for the White Home

We've argued that race neutrality characterises Australia's public sphere in important ways, and the "economic" is one of the principal sites enabling discourses of race neutrality gain legitimacy in society. We showed how the silences about race/racism and the sanctioned forms of public discourses in relation to immigration, international students, and the labour market function to limit understandings of race/racism largely as problems of discrimination. The debate on housing and housing affordability is another important site where the "economic" is framed as race-neutral in Australia. This debate is now happening at a time when cost of living concerns dominate public worries. Housing, which ideally should cost around a quarter of the average individual's income, is the largest cost-of-living expense. This expense, for those paying off a mortgage as well as those renting, is adding increasing pressures on incomes struggling to keep up with the costs of daily living. It was not always like this, commentators say, and worsening housing affordability is a symptom of deeply entrenched economic malaise afflicting Australia's property-obsessed society and economy.

Housing-related household expenses have been rising faster than wages in the urban centres of most rich nations, and this is the outcome of a set of phenomena that started emerging in the late 1960s, through the 1970s, to the current impasse. Briefly: these are the outcome of what is termed "deindustrialisation", i.e., the offshoring of manufacturing out of the rich north to the Global South; the ageing populations of western and other rich societies; the accumulation, in pension funds, of a vast pool of savings and capital in the rich world; the investment of trade surpluses of emerging economies in the rich north etc; this "wall of money" looking for avenues to invest, and finding real estate as a lucrative sector; and the retraction of the welfare state, the ascendance of the "market" in providing for social needs, and the emergence of what is called neo-liberalism leading to the growth of financial deregulation and asset-based welfare. Compared with other advanced industrialised societies, many observers say, Australia is reported to have had relatively rapid house price growth in the last two decades.

For our purposes, we must focus on the framing/s of the housing affordability and homeownership crisis in Australia. It is this framing, like the framing of the discussion/s on immigration, that relegates race to the margins of discussion on society in Australia.

In a series on "housing affordability", *The Sydney Morning Herald*, in an article titled "How the great Australian dream transformed the economy into a house of cards", begins by stating that a dysfunctional housing system is dragging down the Australian economy inflicting "long-term financial and community pain on almost every part of the nation". The article blames poor policies, greed, NIMBYism, and population growth for this quagmire. It then asks if the obsession with housing, and the distortion of the economy that this obsession has caused, is "at the heart of the problems plaguing our cities, our governments and our way of life?"

In the 1960s, the home ownership rate was 70 per cent. Three decades later, in the 1990s, this rate dropped to nearly 43 per cent, and another 28 per cent had a mortgage. Today, less than a third of Australians own their home, 35 per cent hold a mortgage and more than 30 per cent rent. In the 1960s, fewer than one in five people were in the private rental market.

In Australian cities, among the most expensive cities in the world, property prices have been trending upwards for nearly half a century, but salaries have not managed to keep up. These soaring prices have "delivered soaring debt levels and tumbling homeownership rates". Soaring property prices, however, are a windfall for Australians who own their homes outright: it helps them fund their lifestyles in retirement as well as enable their children, through inheritances, maintain the social privileges that come with property ownership.

So, in a society ostensibly based on equal opportunity, inheritance is shaping social destiny: the family home or housing — traditionally seen as a basic human right of shelter or dwelling — has in recent decades transformed into an asset that determines social status, and the nature of equality in society. The distributional effects of housing wealth and its role in structuring inequality in Australia is one of the central concerns in the housing affordability debate.

The concern about rising inequality is dominated by intergenerational disparities in relation to housing and homeownership. Research shows that many prospective homebuyers believe the only way to get into the property market is through inheritance from parents, and the proportion of those tapping into "the bank of mum and dad" has climbed from 15 per cent in the 1980s to more than 40 per cent. Three decades ago, it took about six years to save a 20 per cent deposit for a median-priced home on the nation's east coast, now it takes 14 years to save for a median-priced property's deposit.

With some variation in detail, broadly speaking, these concerns are echoed by a wide cross section of commentators in Australia's public sphere.

Like nostalgia for the golden age of migration to Australia, the politics of remembering and evoking the golden age of housing in Australia hymns the White home and White family life from Australia's recent past. An Australian Housing and Urban Research Institute (AHURI) report says that many baby boomers look back on the 1950s and 1960s as a time when their parents, and later their own households, owned a detached house in the expanding suburbs or regional towns of Australia. These houses were purchased cheaply, with low interest loans, from rising incomes and secure jobs. Neighbourhoods were full of children, and driveways typically had a Holden (an icon of the golden era of Australian manufacturing). The institutional framework behind the economic settings conducive to high homeownership rates for three decades, from the 1940s to the seventies, changed dramatically in the 1980s and 1990s rendering the housing system of those years unfeasible. The fading of this era was the outcome of a changed social landscape that structurally transformed Australia's housing system. Experts say that there is little chance of Australia maintaining the high levels of homeownership of the past, and structural trends towards different rates of declines in homeownership, for different groups of households, are likely to remain into the future.

Many observers refer to the institutional environment that enabled the Australian dream to come into existence and remind us of the changed socio-economic circumstances that we live in today. The institutional environment of a society shapes urban form, the labour market, and financial systems, and through these the distribution of income and wealth. The institutional environment also includes "the values, structures and mechanisms of social order and cooperation". Institutions include legal frameworks, market mechanisms, cultural values and political processes, geography, environmental conditions, and demographic attributes that shape a country's housing system. Institutions shape the nature and the culture of homeownership, which in turn influences institutional imperatives and decisions. Australia now has an institutional environment which no longer supports home ownership as it did in the past.

The changed institutional scenario includes demographic changes and a changed labour market characterised by higher incomes but greater precarity. The biggest change impacting housing in Australia, as in comparable societies, is considered the deregulation of the financial system. Before deregulation got underway in the 1980s, housing was insulated from the effects of the financial system.

It is common to hear commentators trace the origins of the housing affordability crisis to financial deregulation. This deregulation of the banking and financial system is seen as ushering in the conditions for homes to be commodified, i.e., the financialisation of housing which led to the transformation of homes to real estate assets. In this same period, Australia's labour market and immigration system underwent significant changes impacting urban land values and urban form.

Housing as ethnocentrism, and the story of financialisation

These arguments that stress the role of housing as dwelling, as a fundamental human right that transcends other historical developments like globalisation, are moral arguments as much as anything else. They are also powerful forms of ethnocentrisms, rooted in the ethno-history of societies like Australia, in the sense that ideas of housing and home ownership from what is perceived as the golden era of White Australia, continue to shape ideas and debates about housing.

The story is that increased financialisation potentially enabled more people to borrow to buy houses (ownership), more people borrow to invest in housing (rental investors), and there is also a greater ability for households to buy more expensive housing (trading up), as well as a greater ability for households to borrow more against equity in their homes for non-housing related consumption. One important consequence of financialisation was the relaxed lending conditions, including lower deposits, longer lending periods, and new financial products. Households are now taking on debt on a scale unimaginable in the more regulated era, and this higher level of borrowing leads to substantially higher volumes of money chasing after property, pushing property prices to unprecedented heights. An interesting development here is the changing trends of homeownership driven by financialisation: for example, in 1987, investment lending for new construction accounted for 60 per cent of total housing finance commitments, but by 2014 it was down to 7 per cent. This indicates that most investors are competing for existing property. Research shows that despite massive investment, the shortage of rental stock to relative need (particularly at the low-cost end) has worsened over time. Investment thus has led to house price inflation as investors outbid purchasers and the consequent deterioration of affordability creates more renters, and so drives more investment in rentals, favouring those who are able to use already-accumulated equity. This entrenching cycle results in the accentuation of the property wealth divide and an increase in political influence of landlords.

Race and the asset economy

Let us summarise the above to set the boundaries for what is to follow: the housing affordability crisis is a global crisis felt most acutely in global cities like New York, LA, London, Toronto, Sydney, Melbourne, etc. These urban centres and the nations they are located in have undergone immense socio-economic restructuring as a consequence of intensifying flows of finance and labour migration, leading to a restructuring of urban form and labour markets. Where societies were built around Fordist manufacturing and relatively protected domestic economies, today a global economy dominated by finance, real estate, and services has transformed the place and function of housing in contemporary society, i.e., from homes to assets. This transformation has deeply impacted the political agenda and compulsions in these societies.

It is the prevailing consensus that home ownership has a substantial impact on the distribution of wealth in property-owning democracies. But, in the official public discourses about housing affordability, there is little about race or ethnicity, and how the structural transformation of Australian society is inseparable from changing demographics. In other words, the changed demographic situation is transforming the nature of Australian society, and its institutions. These institutions, we must remember, came together in the golden age of White Australia. We must be attentive to the evasions and silences on the matter of ethnicity/race in public discussions on housing; we must not think that financialisation has no racial implications or logic/s; we must look for the connections that tie the asset economy to White power and privilege.

According to the authors of *The Asset Economy*, the key element shaping inequality today is no longer the employment relationship, but the ability to buy assets that appreciate at a rate faster than inflation and wages. Employment in itself is increasingly incapable of serving as the basis of a middle-class lifestyle. Asset ownership has become more important than employment in determining one's class position in society. And asset appreciation has been engendered by a "specific institutional nexus" that has redrawn Australia's social structure. The division between people who do and do not have access to parental wealth is the faultline shaping the new logic of class.

Who are these people having access to parental wealth? Do they have an ethnicity or race? Are some races greater beneficiaries of intergenerational wealth transfers than other races? And do they hold more property/wealth in Australia? Is this wealth then used to fuel the "rentierisation" of the Australian property sector? And is this rentierisation tied to changing demographics resulting from immigration from the third world? Is this property wealth not related to the patterns of residential segregation we see in Australia? Is this segregation just a matter of people of similar cultures/ethnicities living in proximity, or is there an economic motive behind this segregation?

Let us look briefly at some of the trends behind inheritance: the Productivity Commission, in its 2021 report *Wealth transfers and their economic effects*, says that over $120 billion was passed on in 2018 in wealth transfers, and this figure is more than double that a decade ago. Inheritances account for 90 per cent of all transfers. The online magazine *INTHEBLACK*, discussing the PC report, says most wealth transfers in Australia will be in the form of residential property, unspent super funds and other investment assets bequeathed to family beneficiaries. Baby boomers reportedly will pass on an estimated $224 billion each year in inheritances by 2050. The bank of mum and dad is reported to be the nation's ninth biggest mortgage lender.

So far, with the main themes in the housing affordability debate we have not encountered anything about race and how it structures home ownership and the distributional effects of housing wealth. In fact, it wouldn't be an exaggeration to say that the nature and contours of the debate show that White Australia, through a public sphere dominated by whiteness, speaks about a social issue and its impacts on White Australia, in the process silencing the possibilities for alternate voices through creating the appearance of a universal social problem with a common framework to understand it and come up with solutions.

Let us now move on to the private rental sector (PRS). Recall we said earlier that most investors today are chasing after existing properties, and this is leading to worsening affordability as property prices escalate and it becomes harder for first home buyers to get into the market. This then also forces more and more people to rent. An ABS release says that, according to the 2021 Census, close to 30 per cent of all households rent their home in the private rental market (PRS) — a share that has risen in the past few decades. The 2019/20 Survey of Income and Housing (SIH) showed that renters tend to have lower incomes and spend a larger share of their disposable income on housing costs compared with owner-occupier households (both outright owners and those with a mortgage). The median private renter spends around 26 per cent of their weekly income on rent.

Immigration and the rise in renting

There are about 2.2 million property investors in Australia, and this is around 20 per cent of the population. Tax incentives and the easy availability of credit have made investment properties an attractive proposition to wide sections of the population. From the early 1990s, as mentioned, there has been a structural trend of rising investment in dwellings for private rental. While a quarter of equity investors do not have loans outstanding against these properties, most property investors have debt secured against rental properties. The volume of lending to rental investors has registered considerable increases since the early 1990s. Recent figures show that rental investors make up 30 per cent of all property purchase for residential use. Investing in low-grade stock of established apartment buildings has become an established trend in the property investment sector. More than any other demographic changes in the population, like the rise of younger households, and lone-person households, the rise of the PRS is an outcome of increased levels of immigration. The majority of investors in the PRS are individuals, and in local parlance they are called "mum and dad investors" (not landlords).

The strategy of these landlords is to accumulate homeownership capital gains without being an owner occupier, and rental losses are offset against income tax through negative gearing. Studies have shown that the immigrant gateway cities like Sydney have large concentrations of renters with a spatial concentration of low-rent PRS dwellings in suburbs like Parramatta, Auburn, and Warwick Farm. Something like 11 per cent of Sydney's suburbs have been classified as disadvantaged by researchers, and there are attempts to understand the links between the geography of private rental investment and geographies of socio-economic disadvantage in urban areas.

Higher house prices have a flow-on effect on renting, and lead to rising rents in capital cities and elsewhere. With renting becoming a reality for increasing numbers of people, the distributional effects of increasing house prices are recognised as a problem. Most commentators speak of renting in terms of Generation Rent, which refers to young Australians who either choose to or are forced to live in rental accommodation due to escalating homeownership costs. However, the largest number of renters, and the growth in renting, is happening due to immigration into the gateway cities.

The concentration of new home-building activity too is in suburbs with large numbers of immigrants. For example, in May 2021 *The Sydney Morning Herald* reported that more than 150,000 dwellings were forecast to be built across Sydney by 2025, but out of Sydney's 782 suburbs, more than a quarter of them will be untouched by these developments. The suburbs with the highest growth were forecast to be Parramatta (4305 homes), Marsden Park (3760), and Rouse Hill (2965). These suburbs are well known for high concentrations of recent and established immigrant communities from the Global South. Areas forecast to have zero new developments include Cheltenham, North Epping, Riverview, West Pymble, South Turramurra, East Lindfield, East Killara, Davidson, North Wahroonga, and Killarney Heights. More than half of all new homes in the period to 2025 are projected to be built in just 41 of Sydney's 782 suburbs, the report says.

Demand and supply

The shortage of homes, and the problems around supply and stock, is seen as a major contributing factor in the affordability crisis. Escalating house prices is held to be the outcome of supply bottlenecks. Writing about the problems of supply, Peter Tulip argues that enough apartments are not being built, and much of the current building is happening in the wrong place. The solution is to set and enforce housing targets for local councils. Local-level planning restrictions limit land use, height, lot size, floor area etc. Local councils are held to be biased against development and promote the interests of residents who are against development for reasons including the protection of their property values and the need for social segregation, which has an ethnic dimension too.

And another observer, Tony Richards, writing in the *Australian Financial Review*, says that in 1981, the total number of private dwellings was higher than would have been implied just by the growth in the population in the 40 years since the 1961 census. However, since the start of this century, that growth in the number of dwellings had declined sharply. The slowing in the growth of housing stock was observed in all eight states and territories, and, if the relation between population growth and housing stock remained steady, Australia would've had around 1.3 million more dwellings than the 10.85 million reported in the 2021 census. According to Richards, the slowdown and shortfall in housing stock over the past two decades is surprising given the overall economic conditions; the conclusion is that supply inflexibility is crippling construction of new dwellings.

We must bring to bear the above observations on our concerns related to White spaces, White homes, and the housing affordability problem. We must see if the evidence suggests connections between the symbolic and material value of White spaces, residential segregation, and the housing affordability crisis.

Race and the politics of dwelling

The residential is political, argue David Madden and Peter Marcuse in *In Defence of Housing*. The housing system is always shaped by struggles between different groups in society. The role of social divides and antagonisms in shaping the nature of dwelling is often underemphasised. Madden and Marcuse say that the provision of adequate housing is seen as a technical problem that could be managed well through better construction technology, more homeownership, better zoning and land regulation, and smarter planning. But, they argue, the housing crisis goes deeper than all this, and is the outcome of deeper simultaneous social conflicts. Most immediately, the conflict is between housing as lived social space and housing as an instrument for profitmaking, i.e., a conflict between housing as home and as real estate. The housing crisis, then, stems from the inequalities and antagonisms of class society.

So here we have it again, in some shape or form these commentators all take the problem of housing back to the problem of a class divide, which fundamentally shapes all inequality, including inequalities stemming from housing, in society.

We must pause here to bring in briefly our own concerns about the nature of this debate. Firstly, let us ask if it is possible to abstract or excise home ownership, housing, or dwelling from the history of race relations in Australia? Is it possible to view the history of home ownership in Australia as race neutral? And why is it necessary to recollect and reminisce about the Australian home in a race neutral manner when housing in Australia always had the ethno-racial and cultural stamp of whiteness on it? If, as Adkins et al. say, that asset ownership is becoming more important than employment, where does that leave our arguments in the previous chapter about the labour market and its role in reproducing the racial hierarchy, i.e., whiteness, in Australia? When we look at Australia's urban labour markets, do we have sufficient grounds to think that homes are not connected to work and the professions? As *The Asset Economy* says, a specific institutional nexus created the conditions for asset appreciation; this specific institutional nexus came out of a specific institutional history that made mass homeownership a reality. Our question about the role of race, in this history of mass homeownership and the institutional nexus that drives it today, remains. Of course, it is not possible to make generalisations about home ownership in Australia. There are important differences in housing markets, differences of region, class, culture, age, and more. And it would be stretching things too far to say that a particular logic of race, say whiteness, is a common thread throughout Australia's varied residential landscape. But in trying to think about race, race relations, and homeownership, we must bring together — as urban scholars do (or most often, in Australia, do not) —

immigration, labour markets, the professions, and residential settlement patterns; we must try to see if urban form is simply about capitalism or neo-liberalism, or if the logics of race structure the neo-liberal Australian city.

To discuss settlement patterns and the labour markets of all Australian cities would, of course, be the best way to come up with a picture of the many variables that shape race/ethnicity, settlement and residential patterns, the job market and immigration, but this is beyond the scope of this project. Instead, by focusing on Sydney, the biggest immigrant gateway city, and the city with the largest concentration of immigrant communities, we could get useful insights into race and the production of urban space in Australia.

Works referred to

1. Wetzstein, Steffen. 2017. *The global urban housing affordability crisis*, Urban Studies.
2. https://www.smh.com.au/politics/federal/how-the-great-australian-dream-transformed-the-economy-into-a-house-of-cards-20230407-p5cywt.html?collection=p5d2m8
3. Burke, Terry, Hayward, David. 1992. *Australian Housing at the Crossroads? Built Environment* Alexandrine Press.
4. Adkins, Lisa, Cooper, Melinda, Konings, Martijn. 2020. *The Asset Economy*, Polity.
5. Yates, Judith. 2011, *Housing in Australia in the 2000s: On the agenda too late?* RBA, Annual conference.
6. Williams, Peter. 2015. *The affordable housing conundrum: shifting policy approaches in Australia*, The Town Planning Review.
7. Ryan-Collins, J. and Murray, C. 2020. *When homes earn more than jobs: the rentierization of the Australian housing market.* UCL Institute for Innovation and Public Purpose, Working Paper Series (IIPP WP 2020-08). Available at: https://www.ucl.ac.uk/bartlett/public-purpose/wp2020-08
8. Burke, T., Nygaard C., Ralston L. 2020. *Australian home ownership: past reflections, future directions*, AHURI Final Report 328, Australian Housing and Urban Research Institute Limited, Melbourne, https://www.ahuri.edu.au/research/final-

reports/328, doi: 10.18408/ahuri-5119801.
9. Productivity Commission 2021, *Wealth transfers and their economic effects*, Research paper, Canberra
10. https://intheblack.cpaaustralia.com.au/economy/great-intergenerational-wealth-transfer-explained
11. Pawson, H. & Herath, S. (2015). *Disadvantaged places in urban Australia: residential mobility, place attachment and social exclusion.* AHURI Final Report, 243 1-81.
12. Tulip, Peter, *Where should we build new housing — Better targets for local councils*, Anaysis Paper 45, The Centre for Independent Studies
13. AFR. May 2023. (https://www.afr.com/politics/federal/how-to-solve-australia-s-housing-crisis-20230502-p5d4w9?fbclid=IwAR1_EyW2seUF1UyP4O2SwCNVo7Ck7hI-AgXPk5T61fh81N9E81N7eslj4ol)
14. Marcuse, Peter, Madden, David. 2016. *In Defence of Housing*, Verso.
15. Doling, John, Ronald, Richard *Home ownership and asset-based welfare Journal of Housing and the Built Environment*, June 2010, Vol. 25, No. 2.
16. https://www.smh.com.au/national/nsw/there-will-be-150-000-new-homes-in-sydney-in-four-years-more-than-200-suburbs-will-get-none-of-them-20210505-p57p25.html

9

The Latté Line

In everyday conversations it is assumed that Sydney is a diverse city that people from all around the world call "home". It is also the racial commonsense* in Sydney that there are affluent/White suburbs, and regions and suburbs that are largely immigrant, i.e., non-White. So, for instance, non-White people are sometimes, or often, assumed to live in the western suburbs of Sydney; White Australians and many other western Europeans are seen as living closer to the city or the choicest locations of the city. Sydney's 782 suburbs are not by any means monoracial, but the patterns of immigrant settlement and the residential dynamics that keep neighbourhoods and areas of suburbs White are instructive. The logics of keeping the ethnic make-up of a suburb or a neighbourhood largely homogenous, or neighbourhoods where one ethnicity or culture predominates, applies to non-White communities too. However, if cultural difference or ethnic homogeneity were the reasons for groups of co-ethnics clustering together in diverse regions of the city, as the "racial commonsense" dictates, the contested nature of urban space and the knowledge we have about these urban conflicts would not be problematic. In other words, reducing the struggle for urban space as the unfolding of race neutral neoliberal urbanisation and its logics of gentrification, suburbanisation, or sprawl is a powerful strategy to silence discussion about the compulsions of racial hegemony that overdetermine the politics of space in Sydney.

It is common to hear urbanists remind us that it is wrong to view space as a container; rather, space is the outcome of social struggles and investments. We could put this another way and say that the spaces of the city are coded with the ethno-racial culture/s and social mores of the various groups that use and frequent these spaces for a multiplicity of purposes. Such a process of coding and over-coding of urban space could only happen if what is called "economic" and "cultural" were enmeshed in urban spaces that ethnicities/races carve out for their socio-cultural existence. Since economic activity is characterised in today's cities by a great deal of overlapping and interconnection between, say an ethnic enclave, with a concentration of ethnic enterprises and informal work, and the apparatus of local government, and through these connections with urban administrators and mainstream businesses, the nature of urban space and its usage is ethno-racially diversified. This is to say that it would be futile to look for a space that is Asian or White in a homogenous manner, just as it would be futile to look for a residential area that is populated by just one ethnicity, since the housing stock in every residential area is varied by density, age, and proximity to commercial centres. So, to state the obvious, factors like class, i.e., economic status, ethnicity, profession, age, and cultures that correspond to a mix of these elements go to determine residential choices and patterns.

Through all this diversity in urban residential and commercial spaces we must trace the compulsions of racial hegemony and its need to differentiate itself through a politics of urban territoriality. This is not uncomplicated and is bound to break down beyond a point since culture, race, economy, and work have interconnections that cannot be disentangled or traced back to a single homogenous source or unifying factor or social group. However, if we want to gain an appreciation of the politics of White hegemony and its complex investments that reshape it even as it shapes them, we need to pursue White spaces and examine their contours and becomings in an urban setting fragmented and polarised by immigration, transnationalism, and race.

Space, race, and the social divide in Sydney

Let us begin by asking the question, often implicit in discussions on immigration and diversity: Is Sydney polarised along the lines of race? If so, how does this polarisation manifest, spatially and socially? How can we understand this socio-spatial divide by looking at immigration, housing, ethno-racial settlement patterns, and the labour market/s of Sydney? Could we say that the perception and narrative/s of a crisis that manifest in the socio-spatial ordering of the city is based on older/traditional understandings of what a society is supposed to look like? In other words, are the traditional ideas we have of society, shaped by ethnic and cultural homogeneity and far less racial diversity, adequate in helping us understand social processes in a global metro? Is this socio-spatial divide a consequence of homophily, people of similar cultural and economic circumstances living and working together, in proximity? Or is this divide produced through everyday individual and collective actions enabled by the institutions of contemporary multicultural Australia? Is the divide an outcome of residential and labour market segregation? If segregation is at play in the housing and job market/s how does it operate in a time of increasing diversity and multiculturalism?

In thinking of these phenomena and the problems associated with them, the literature in Australia seems to be around an either/or debate: the first is that Australia is not like America; it has a vibrant, healthy ethnic mosaic. The other extreme is something like: we are a divided society, and that divide is a consequence of rising levels of immigration and racial/cultural differences. We must move away from this either/or framework and try to come up with alternate understandings of urban space, and its divides and disparities.

The largest concentrations of immigrant populations in Sydney are in the western suburbs of Sydney (GWS). Large communities of immigrants from the Global South live in many other parts of the city, but the west of Sydney is regarded as predominantly non-White and immigrant, and much of the population growth here has occurred in the last three decades. GWS's population is 2,654,467 (ABS 2022). More than half the population growth in Sydney for much of the last decade has been concentrated in the western suburbs of the city, and immigration from overseas is the main driver of this growth in the western suburbs. The 13 western Sydney local government areas (LGAs) include: the City of Canterbury Bankstown, Blacktown City, Blue Mountains City, Camden Council, Campbelltown City, Fairfield City, Hawkesbury City, Holroyd, Liverpool City, City of Parramatta, Penrith City, The Hills Shire, and Wollondilly Shire. The largest ancestries are Australian (520,888), English (476,834), Chinese (231,571), Indian (171,170), Irish (130,348), Lebanese (129,913), Scottish (107,376), Italian (96,841), Vietnamese (94,371), and Filipino (89,445). 177,599 people have no stated ancestry. The category 'Australian' includes first- and second-generation immigrants who identify as Australian, as well as White Australians. Increasing levels of migration from the Asian region has meant that the Chinese, Indian, and Filipino communities are registering the fastest rates of growth in this area.

A 2015 report by the Centre for Western Sydney (CWS), *Work, Places and People in Western Sydney*, looks at data on total income in the area (GWS), which, the report says, is an indication of how much money is available on average for people to live on: *"The lowest income (the limit for this quintile being $22,000 per annum) areas in Sydney occupy a corridor bounded roughly by the Great Western Highway and Canterbury Rd through Sydney's outer west and southwest, following the Hume Highway to Campbelltown LGA. The ATO data show a clear inequality line in Greater Sydney, roughly along a fold in the map from the city's northwest (The Hills LGA) to the southeast (Sutherland Shire). The inverse of the lower income districts to the south and west of this fold are the deep green postcodes* *of Sydney's north shore suburbs running from The Hills to Chatswood and Warringah, across Sydney harbour to its eastern suburbs. The high-income quintile commences at $45,000 per resident and extends to $120,000 per resident. Between the highest and the lowest quintiles are three intermediate categories between $22,000 and $45,0000 which create an orderly social slope of income inequality across the city".*

Data from the latest census (2021) on the ABS website show similar patterns: household income levels for the Western Sydney LGA compared to Greater Sydney show that there was a smaller proportion of high-income households (those earning $3,000 per week or more) and a higher proportion of low-income households (those earning less than $800 per week). Overall, 24.8 per cent of the households earned a high income and 19.2 per cent were low-income households, compared with 30.1 per cent and 17.9 per cent respectively for Greater Sydney.**

Work, Places and People in Western Sydney says that Western Sydney's growth has been largely driven by the growing population, but the area has had a *"rising deficiency of employment opportunities relative to the growth-rates of resident labour forces in inner LGAs of GWS such as Bankstown, Blacktown, Fairfield and Holroyd. While employment still grew faster than resident labour forces in most outer LGAs, GWS's inner LGAs remain job-deficit areas".* The report states labour force participation rates are well below those of eastern and northern Sydney. Incomes work much harder in these areas, and there are higher concentrations of workers in sectors and occupations with lower wages. The region also has greater proportions of workers who are poorly qualified or lack relevant experience, and/or are forced into precarious labour market segments.

In the years between 2015 and 2022, the Centre for Western Sydney followed up with more research reports on the labour market and the economy of western Sydney, calling attention to the continuing shortage of jobs for local residents, and the concentration of precarious and low-wage blue collar jobs in GWS. These reports also point to the growing population as one of the factors behind the growth of the regional economy, and the inability of the region's job market to provide adequate employment. It is important to mention here that GWS's affordable housing has been a factor in attracting immigrants from overseas, as well as local migrants in need of more affordable housing options.

The construction of new homes in western Sydney is a big part of the story behind the area's economic growth — construction itself is one of the largest employers in the region. Western Sydney has consistently had higher rates of home completions than other parts of Sydney. Further, the large immigrant communities in GWS have socio-cultural investments in the west that make the western suburbs more than just a laggard or neglected economic powerhouse. In other words, the non-White immigrant communities and their vibrant socio-cultural lives have transformed the place and weight of the western suburbs in Sydney's and Australia's political and cultural landscape. This is also an important story of placemaking, belonging, and "assimilation" through housing and community building. One could say that the areas known for their large concentrations of immigrant populations like Kellyville, Blacktown, Bankstown, Westmead, and Pendle

Hill are examples of what segregation scholars term "spatial assimilation", and "community building".

Housing, work, and the latté line

The debate on housing supply and affordability is instructive in relation to the location of housing and its relation to jobs. This framing of the connections of housing to labour markets stresses the economic, social, and environmental costs of not having adequate housing supply close to the highest concentration of jobs in the city. A good example of this argument about the disconnect between housing and access to jobs is a 2018 article in *The Conversation*. The article *Another tale of two cities: access to jobs divides Sydney along the 'latté line'*, says that Sydney's "latté line" divides the city in two by jobs. The authors of the article say that their research shows residents are segregated by "overall access to jobs and access to white-collar jobs. This highlights the jobs inequality underlying residential segregation". The white-collar jobs are concentrated in the north and east of the city (above the latté line), and the blue collar jobs are mostly in the south and west (below the latté line). The article argues that the cost of this spatial mismatch is borne by residents below the latté line in higher commuting costs. "The latté line roughly starts from Sydney International Airport and extends towards Parramatta, and then up to the north-west region. The line generally indicates a socio-economic division between the north-eastern and south-western regions of metropolitan Sydney." The article mentions the uneven distribution of jobs in the metropolitan region, and shows that white-collar jobs are concentrated on one side of the latté line and blue collar jobs on the other side. Among the solutions suggested are better transport connectivity for people in the western suburbs of Sydney.

To give one more illustrative example of the narrative of crisis and the spatial divide in Sydney, an article in The Conversation, NIMBYism in Sydney is leading to racist outcomes says, "Residents of the affluent east and north of Greater Sydney have strongly resisted housing developments in their suburbs. This NIMBY (Not in My Back Yard) resistance has led to urban sprawl in areas of Western Sydney". According to the article, ethnic segregation is a less-talked-about aspect of this divide. It says that the growth in Sydney's population is mostly from non-White new immigrants, and NIMBYism leads to "dumping" these new immigrants in the city's west, creating an ethnically segregated city. The inner-city areas have the largest concentrations of White residents and are forecast to have the least housing development, effectively excluding non-White people who need to be in areas closer to jobs. Among the areas listed as low in racial diversity (less than 10 per cent non-White residents) are the wealthiest suburbs of Sydney like Woollahra, Waverly, Northern Beaches, Mosman, and Sutherland Shire. Areas with 10 to 20 per cent non-White residents include the inner-west. Central Sydney has a non-White population that is 26.22 per cent of the residents.

White spaces, White work

The articles cited above give us an indication of the framing of the socio-spatial divide of the city of Sydney. Some questions we must raise about immigrants and the labour market in GWS at this point: are non-White immigrants confined to the suburbs of western Sydney? If they are dispersed throughout other areas of the city, are there patterns we can discern in relation to their housing/settlement patterns, and labour market engagement? If low-wage blue collar work is concentrated in western Sydney, are the low-wage sectors of GWS dominated by non-White workers? What percentage of the non-White workforce is in better paying jobs? Is this disparity — the preponderance of non-White workers in low-wage jobs — a consequence of lack of skills and education; or work and residency rights; or a mix of these? Is it the labour market status of the communities living in the western suburbs that determines their residential choice in the area? If the percentage of high-wage earners in the western suburbs are mostly White Australians, or those who are acculturated to the local culture, and/or those with education and skills, could we then, as we explained earlier, assume that race/ethnicity and an associated culture determine income and wealth? Conversely, could we say that non-White immigrants are spatially sorted to suburbs that are economically and culturally at a remove from areas of the city that are synonymous with the image of White Australia? Is this pattern of spatial distance between non-White immigrants and White Australians in the labour and housing markets evident in other areas of Sydney? If so, how? Does diversity and multiculturalism blur the social divides, or do they work with the divide, complementing and reinforcing it? What can that tell us about the racialised socio-spatial structure of the city? To gain an appreciation of this complex and contradictory picture of social and spatial distances in Sydney, we must look again at the data for individual suburbs and LGAs, and see if we can come up with a picture that corresponds to our ideas about a caste order and its social compulsions.

The problem with the latté line

The common characterisations, in the media and academic research, of the ethno-racial divide that structures the socio-spatial divide in Sydney is general and simplistic in many ways. Firstly, as mentioned, non-White immigrant clusters are spread all over the city. Surely, the wealthiest suburbs have the smallest concentrations of non-Whites, especially immigrants. However, in most suburbs in Sydney, racial diversity is on the rise, and this diversity spans socio-economic classes. This is to say that affluent and middle-class non-White residents are present in an increasing number of suburbs in the city. However, this diversity sometimes veils the fact that the highest incomes and wealth are always concentrated in suburbs and neighbourhoods that are majority White. So, in a suburb with large clusters of immigrants, the best locations, neighbourhoods, and streets are still majority-White. The diversity that surrounds majority-White neighbourhoods and streets gives the impression of overall diversity. What is important to keep in mind here, and what needs to be substantiated with data on housing and suburban demographics, is that the "latté line" that divides Sydney's suburbs along the lines of class and race is not straightforward. In other words, this line, or this spatiality of high income, wealth, and its correlation with race, is a social phenomenon that manifests in many locations of the city, as a structural social trend or reality.

Second, such a characterisation of a general socio-spatial divide is based on a false and misleading picture of immigration and labour markets. In other words, this idea of non-White immigrants living far from jobs in the city hides the picture of how high-wage and low-wage jobs cluster together in locations with high concentrations of jobs, like in CBDs. It could easily be shown that the high wage jobs in any location tend to predictably have a higher proportion of White workers, and the low wage jobs tend to have a substantially higher proportion of non-White workers. This means that jobs, wages, and sectors of employment may have tendencies to aggregate in certain parts of a city, but equally the segmentation of the labour market along the lines of race/ethnicity does not respect any locational boundaries or urban economic geographies as described by Australian social scientists. These are points we mentioned at the outset of this discussion. The nature of social space in Sydney, and the role race plays in it, will be elaborated as we go along.

Coming back to housing and GWS, the availability of houses and the opportunity to own a home is a big drawcard for large numbers of immigrants, especially "skilled" immigrants from Asia. The chance of owning a home in Australia, it is well known, is high on the list of immigrant aspirations, and home ownership is an important stage in the "assimilation of immigrants". It is also a well-known strategy for immigrants to improve their financial status in the asset economy. Several reports in the media have pointed to the high numbers of immigrants purchasing homes in greenfield developments in the outer suburbs. It would be no exaggeration to argue that urban sprawl would not happen without immigration-driven population growth, and this means that housing in the outer suburbs drives the asset economy of Australia in ways that cannot be underestimated.

Combined as a whole, the number of non-White ethnicities living in the outer suburbs are the majority in this region. In that sense, looking beyond individual suburbs, we could say that the general picture of the western suburbs is one of a "majority minority" area. The trend of immigrants flocking to new developments in the outer suburbs, leading to sprawl, is well-known, and is often described as economically and environmentally inefficient. It is important, though, to mention here that more than half the residential properties completed in Sydney in recent decades are apartments in and around the inner and middle suburbs of Sydney. Both of these trends — the construction of new homes in the western suburbs, and the construction of apartments in the middle and inner suburbs of the city — are tied to demographic change resulting from immigration and immigrant residential settlement patterns. These trends are also a reflection of the changing labour market requirements of a growing global metropolis.

As mentioned, immigrants are present in large clusters in many locations in the inner ring of the city. In many suburbs with large concentrations of non-White people there are, of course, both owners and renters among the non-White residents. However, there are also evidently patterns of lower socio-economic clusters that we see in many suburbs in the inner city where large numbers of non-White immigrants live in affordable older apartments (low-grade stock) closer to shops, town centres, transport hubs, and industrial areas. Representative of these suburbs are Lakemba, Wiley Park, Punchbowl, Campsie, Burwood, Croydon, Ashfield, Strathfield, Belmore, Auburn, Flemington, and Homebush. The list of these suburbs would be so long that it would make the subject of a book devoted to discussing immigrant clusters and their residential patterns in these areas. The point here is that the socio-spatial divide is not as simple as what the "latté line" would have us believe. Additionally, the significant changes in immigration that we discussed earlier have made fundamental changes to immigrant settlement and residential patterns in Sydney.

Apartment living and immigration

The story of the growth of apartment living in Australia and in Sydney is the story of changing demographics driven by immigration from the Global South. We could say, then, that immigrant settlements across the greater Sydney region follow a path described commonly in the past as new migrants settling closer to work in affordable rentals, and, as their socio-economic situation improves over the years, the tendency is for them to transition to ownership. This is the well-known narrative of immigration and settlement in settler societies. However, when we look at the dispersed nature of immigrant communities across the entire city, and the changing composition of immigrants from permanent skilled migrants to temporary migration and international students, we see the close connection of migration-driven demographic changes and the growth of apartment living in Sydney. While reports in the media and research reveal that apartment living is on the rise, a closer look at who lives in apartments, the quality of apartments, where they are located, and what the trends in apartment construction tell us, it becomes evident that the latté line is an oversimplification of a complex socio-spatial divide in Sydney.

The shortage of apartments

The boom in construction of apartments closer to the city, however, falls significantly short of the demand for high density housing closer to the CBD and its labour markets. The Urban Development Institute of Australia's (UDIA) *2022 Apartment Supply Pipeline Report* estimates that NSW has a shortage of 48,000 apartments, and this shortage is set to grow. The report says that historically two-thirds of the supply of new homes in NSW has been apartments, and a healthy apartment sector is critical to tackling the housing shortage. Apartment rentals are particularly critical to the well-being of people on low incomes in NSW, adds the report.

In its 2016 population census data, the ABS says that more and more Australians are taking up apartment living. In 2016, 10 per cent of all people in Australia lived in an apartment, and that figure was higher in NSW, with Sydney, the largest immigrant gateway, reporting by far the largest number of apartment dwellers. In the 25 years to 2016, the number of occupied apartments in Australia increased by 78 per cent. The figures for the year 2021 are higher: some estimates say 15 per cent of Sydney's population lives in apartments, others estimate it to be 22 per cent (19.9 per cent on the ABS site). Whatever the right figure, a substantial portion of Sydney's population are apartment dwellers. An ABC report on the 2021 census says about 45 per cent (247,506) of high-rise apartment dwellers are in Greater Sydney, where there are nearly 120,000 apartments, or 32 per cent of the national total. Many of these high-rise apartments are in suburbs with large numbers of immigrants. Sydney has 35,889 high rise homes, Parramatta 13,955, Bayside 10,682, North Sydney 7,826, Ryde 6,380, Willoughby 4,893, Canada Bay 4,353, Georges River 3,080, Liverpool 3,321, and Cumberland 2,395.

It is not clear what the exact area termed "Sydney" refers to in the ABC report cited above on high rise apartments. If we go by the area on the idcommunity profile (https://profile.id.com.au/sydney/about), Sydney is bounded by Port Jackson in the north, the Woollahra Municipal Council area and Randwick City in the east, the Bayside Council area in the south, and the Inner West Council area in the west. This area has a population of 217,748; 31 per cent of households were purchasing or fully owned their home, 53.75 per cent were renting privately, and 6.8 per cent were in social housing in 2021. 97 per cent of dwellings here are medium or high density: 19.9 per cent are medium, and 77.1 per cent high density. 34.8 per cent used a language other than English at home. In the following, we will try to use the data to show the close connection between high-density living and non-English speaking people.

Renting: high-density living and non-English speakers

Given the proximity to high income jobs and the clustering of professional jobs and the knowledge economy, financial, and creative sectors in this part of the city, it should come as no surprise that English speakers dominate the residential population of this area. However, people born overseas form a majority in the City of Sydney. If we look at the area Sydney, within the City of Sydney: we see that in a population of 17,451, 60.3 per cent used a language other than English at home, 98 per cent of dwellings in this area are medium or high density, and 66.8 per cent are renting privately. If we look at another area in the City of Sydney dominated by non-White immigrants, Ultimo, we see the trend of renting dominant here (58.1 per cent). The City of Sydney is the area with the largest concentration of jobs, and, besides, it is close to the wealthiest White areas of the city. Hence, it is not an ideal sample to try to trace the effects of the "latté line" along an ethnic/racial pattern. However, the pattern of race, wealth, income, and economic opportunity as shaped by ethno-racial factors would reveal itself if more data on race/ethnicity, occupation, and tenure type were available.

Let us look at some other areas of high rise living: Parramatta, Bayside, Ryde, Georges River, and Liverpool. Every suburb has its own characteristics determining the mix of residents there, and these include the type of housing stock and availability, access to jobs, and the presence of schools and amenities. These factors determine the mix of White and non-White residents.

The City of Parramatta has 63.2 per cent medium or high-density dwellings, and 56.4 per cent of the population used a language other than English at home. This indicates a higher rate of high-density living occurs with higher rates of non-English speaking, non-White populations. In Bayside Council area, 51.5 per cent used a language other than English at home, 66.5 per cent of dwellings were medium or high rise; in the City of Ryde 60.9 per cent of the dwellings were medium or high density, and this area has more than 50 per cent of the resident population speaking a language other than English at home. In the Georges River area, 49.4 per cent dwellings are medium or high density, and 53.2 per cent of the resident population speaks a language other than English at home. In Liverpool, 77.3 per cent dwellings were medium or high density, and 64.9 per cent used a language other than English at home. If we change the area that comes under a council or LGA (local government area) these figures of course will change, as high-density living is usually closer to the transport nodes and commercial centres. So, for instance, Liverpool LGA will have a lower percentage of people using a language other than English at home (53.8 per cent) compared to the Liverpool CBD (64.9 per cent), and a lower percentage of people living in medium or high density (29.2 per cent) compared to 77.3 per cent in the CBD. This pattern will hold for most areas, with medium and high-density living being closer to commercial areas and more non-White residents dominating in apartments; as the dwelling structure changes to stand-alone houses further away from commercial areas, the population mix too would change to proportionately fewer non-Whites. So again, for example, in

Bayside Council, the stock of housing and the residential mix would change with proximity to commercial centres having high-rise and medium density housing with large numbers of non-White residents. This pattern is evident as we move further from the town centre of Kogarah or Rockdale. The same pattern can be seen in almost any area with high rise or medium-density housing close to transport nodes and commercial centres.

Who lives in apartments?

Let us look at what the research tells us about the types of people who live in apartments in Sydney. Research by the UNSW and others reveal that most apartment dwellers in Sydney were not born in Australia, although close to half say they were born in Australia. It is important to bear in mind that born in Australia includes both White and non-White people, although the category mostly comprises White people. English as the main language is only reported by 45 per cent of apartment dwellers. Most apartment dwellers rent, and this is an important point for our argument. Lone-person households make up 31 per cent of apartment dwellers, couples with no children make up 25 per cent, couples with children are 17 per cent, single parents make up 7 per cent, and group households are 8 per cent, and finally there is a group categorised as other (12 per cent). In terms of age, the largest group is people in the 20-39 age group (48 per cent), people aged between 40-59 are 21 per cent of apartment dwellers, those under 20 years make up 16 per cent, and those over the age of 60 make up 15 per cent. We could assume that large numbers of recent immigrants would make up the couples with no children category, being recent immigrants, and immigrants and non-White people would also dominate the category couples with children. The real break-up of all these cohorts would only be possible with more ethnicity related data, which is not available.

Race and the private rental sector

Research into the geography of private rental housing in Australia shows that there is a growing role for private rental, and in recent decades the private rental sector has been showing higher rates of growth than other tenures. There are rising numbers of long-term renters, which is paralleled by an expanding cohort of investor landlords. Housing finance for investor landlord acquisitions are also rapidly growing. The private rental sector in Australia is reported to be growing at the expense of home ownership, and this is seen to be a consequence of demographic change, including smaller households, rising numbers of immigrant workers, and/ or students. In this context, research also calls attention to the suburbanisation of poverty in urban Australia, marking a decisive shift away from the inner city. There is also a growing trend towards the spatial concentration of low-rent dwellings in Sydney. The geography of private rental expansion in relation to neighbourhood disadvantage too is important here: research shows that for the years 2006-2014 there was a disproportionate growth of private rentals in "disadvantaged" suburbs. For the period under study, 11 per cent of Sydney's suburbs were classed as "disadvantaged". These disadvantaged suburbs were predominantly in the middle and outer suburbia. For the period 2006-2014, private rentals were down from 31 per cent to 29 per cent of total, and in the outer suburbs they were up from 34 per cent to 35 per cent. Although this figure is a decade old now, it indicates a shift towards the outer suburbs of Sydney of low-cost private rentals (*Exploring the geography of Australia's private rental investment boom*, Hal Pawson, Kath Hulse, Bill Randolph).

The landlord as property investor, and the non-White tenant

In relation to the growth of the private rental sector, an important point for our argument is the role of the property investor and landlord. While traditionally viewed negatively, today landlords are widely considered to be "mum and dad" investors. Property investment is also seen to accumulate wealth through capital gains, and as a financial strategy that enables investors to deduct losses, through negative gearing, on their entire taxable income. Around 20 per cent of Australia's 11.4. million taxpayers owned an investment property, and 71.48 per cent of investors hold one investment property, 18.86 per cent hold two investment properties, 5.81 per cent own three investment properties, 2.11 per cent own four investment properties, 0.87 per cent own five investment properties, and 0.89 per cent (19,920) hold six or more properties.

Next to nothing has been said in Australia about the nexus between a growing population of low-wage workers from the Global South and property investment. In other words, property investment relies on rental income, and a great deal of investment in rental properties is in the apartment sector housing non-White non-English speaking immigrants. Investors may, of course, be from all races, as it is open to anyone with the means to invest in the property market. However, the discursive framing of a "generation rent" has led to the perception that all renters face the same hurdles in the rental market. Public discussion, even by organisations advocating for tenant rights, gives the impression that race-neutral processes determine rental market dynamics. However, when one looks at the concentration of non-White people in affordable low-grade apartment stock, it becomes hard not to conclude that racial steering is prevalent in the Australian rental market. Many studies in Australia have pointed to racial discrimination in the rental market. However, these studies are silent about the collective institutional nature of this social process behind the preponderance of ethnic groups of recent immigrants and middle- and low-income non-White groups clustering in low-grade apartment stock. While there is ethnic diversity in streets and neighbourhoods with medium density apartments, the percentage of White residents is always low in locations where non-Whites are in a majority.

We now have a reasonable idea of why it is simplistic to think of Sydney's spatial divide as a "latté line", i.e., the west vs the more affluent parts of the city. The reasons for the continuing salience of this discourse of "the west vs the rest" go partly to the traditional conceptions of the economic and social divide of the city. It is not that these discourses are lacking in truth or facts, but that the distribution of income, wealth, and social power are more complex in this era of globalisation, mass migration, and increasing racial and economic diversity. It is strange that commentators still rely on old cultural and social paradigms to make sense of a changed society where the processes of marginalisation or downward mobility, just like upward mobility, cannot be understood through traditional economic geographies. If we go back to the problem we started with (How does housing determine the distribution of income and wealth in Sydney?) it becomes clear, looking at the patterns cited earlier, that we have a complex picture of diversity in Sydney's residential mosaic.

Works referred to
1. Fagan, Robert, O'Neill, Phillip, *Work, places and people in Western Sydney: changing suburban labour markets* 2001-2014, The Centre for Western Sydney (2015)
2. O'Neill, P. 2020. *Where are the jobs? Part 2: The geography of Western Sydney's jobs deficit*, Centre for Western Sydney, Western Sydney University, Parramatta
3. https://theconversation.com/another-tale-of-two-cities-access-to-jobs-divides-sydney-along-the-latte-line-96907
4. https://theconversation.com/nimbyism-in-sydney-is-leading-to-racist-outcomes-207204
5. Morris, Alan, Hulse, Kath, Pawson, Hal *The Private Rental Sector in Australia: Living in Uncertainty Springer* (2021)
6. Nelson, Jacqueline, MacDonald, Heather, Dufty-Jones, Rae, Dunn, Kevin, Paradies, Yin "Ethnic Discrimination in the Private Rental Housing Markets in Australia" in *Housing in 21st-Century Australia: People, Practices and Policies* Routledge
7. *Apartment Supply Pipeline Report (2022)* Urban Development Institute of Australia
8. Pawson, H. & Herath, S. (2015). *Disadvantaged places in urban Australia: residential mobility, place attachment and social exclusion.* AHURI Final Report, 243 1-81.
9. Yates, J., Wulff, M. and Reynolds, M. (2004) *"Changes in the supply of and need for low rent dwellings in the private rental market"* Australian Housing and Urban Research Institute positioning paper www.ahuri.edu.au/global/docs/doc592.pdf
** (https://profile.id.com.au/cws/household-income).
* In *Race for Profit*, Keeanga-Yamahtta Taylor writes about how the US government imported the racial commonsense of the real estate industry in framing its housing policy. *Race for Profit.* 2019. University of North Carolina Press.

10

Immigration and Segregation

It is well known that in choosing a location or suburb, homebuyers always factor in the racial composition of the area as well as the schools in the vicinity, and the racial composition of the schools. Given all this, we must ask if homogeneity is the result of homophily? If so, what is homophily in a time of diversity, and the spaces that are ostensibly designed to enable diversity at work and in social life? Are there any connections we can draw between occupational segregation, residential clustering, and socio-economic status? How much of it is class? And what is the role of race? How do we explain income heterogeneity in same-race neighbourhoods? If so, could we say that race trumps class? Or would that be simplistic? Could we say that the "latté line" points to crucial facts about the labour markets of Sydney: that there are more jobs in the wealthier areas, and the wealthier areas are whiter, and this concentration of jobs, the prevalence of more jobs in whiter areas of the city, is an outcome of economic and racial segregation? Could we then say that, as we argued in previous chapters, that labour markets and work are racialised and segmented off together with residential areas? Can we understand these processes by looking at immigrant pathways to settlement and assimilation?

On the assimilation of immigrants in "host" societies, segregation researchers have two main paradigms that inform research. One is the spatial assimilation model, which says that immigrants assimilate over the years as their socio-economic status improves. As their employment prospects and socio-cultural familiarity improve, immigrants convert these gains into better housing to reflect their improved status and investments in a society. As mentioned earlier, non-White immigrant homeowners can be found in many of Sydney's suburbs, and this makes it difficult to contend that they are confined to GWS. However, data on the actual numbers, and the proportion of non-White homeowners in the better suburbs as well as all other suburbs, would be necessary to come to a fuller understanding of this process of immigrant upward mobility in the different areas of the city. Further, data would also be required on the labour market pathways that led to the "spatial assimilation" of these immigrant homeowners in Sydney. This is because immigrant upward socio-economic mobility has primarily occurred through entrepreneurship in ethnic enclaves and small businesses. This does not mean that the professions have not been a pathway to upward mobility for non-Whites, but the percentage of non-White professionals living in the sought-after suburbs of Sydney could be dwarfed by immigrant entrepreneurs. This is a point to keep in mind when we think about the politics and economics of segregated living and work in contemporary cities.

There are many problems in assuming that diversity in the suburbs means immigrants are assimilating, and there is no segregation. The appearance of diversity, as mentioned, may be related to the geographic scale used in measuring segregation, i.e., a suburb may look diverse but areas and streets within that suburb would show racial groups clustering and marking off their territory from other groups. These residential boundaries may be realised through price mechanisms, stand-alone houses vs medium density, greener and quieter streets closer to better parks, and so on. Such streets and areas may have a history of groups living there for decades, and so continuity may be another factor. Even so, the prevalence of racial or ethnic homogeneity in residential areas or occupations or sectors of the economy in a time of increasing diversity is a social phenomenon that requires closer examination.

Increasing volumes of immigration in recent years, and the growth of temporary migration together with the expansion of the services sector (food, hospitality, retail) has led to diverging pathways of immigrant settlement. This means that it is impossible to generalise across the different phases of immigration, and the settlement patterns of people who migrated to Australia a few decades ago and those who've arrived recently. Since Australia has had a huge immigration program targeting immigrants with tertiary qualifications that enable better labour market outcomes, in addition to other humanitarian settlement programs with different labour market and residential outcomes, both drawing large numbers of immigrants from the Asia region, it would be necessary to look at large sets of data relating to the socio-economic profiles of various immigrant cohorts to determine if better education has led to better spatial assimilation or not.

The second important theory in segregation scholarship is the place stratification model, which holds that discrimination in the housing market means that well-established resident groups use their resources to distance themselves from those they consider outsiders. This is seen as a strategy to keep resources within their own networks, and the result is segregation. We mentioned the prevalence of this in the rental housing market, and the preponderance of ethnic groups in GWS is also viewed as an outcome of segregation. This segregation is also described through discourses like the "latté line" as socio-economic and ethnic, and it argues that better jobs are concentrated in White-dominant areas of the city. So, despite the prevalence of diversity in Sydney's residential areas, we see racial homogeneity at play at the neighbourhood or street level, and often at the suburban scale too.

From all this we get a mixed picture: broadly, this is a scenario of Whites and those who share their socio-economic and cultural characteristics living in proximity. We also have ethnic groups choosing to live within their own ethnic communities, and this trend is evident in GWS where suburbs like Pendle Hill, Kellyville, Toongabbie, and Westmead, to name a few, have large concentrations of co-ethnics speaking the same language and sharing the same neighbourhood or living in proximity. We also have concentrations of Chinese, Vietnamese, Filipinos, and Indians in suburbs from Blacktown to Fairfield. While there would be ethnic diversity in these suburbs, the general pattern is for one ethno-linguistic group to be numerically dominant in an area, and that area, in turn, will reflect through its commercial centres and residential streets the ethno-racial stamp of the group living there. Greenacre is a good case in point. The point here is that space is not marked off or monopolised by just White Australians; rather we see all immigrant groups marking off their territory through their settlement patterns in Sydney. Even within an immigrant ethnic group we find socio-economic heterogeneity, with people higher up the economic ladder living in better parts of the suburb. Chester Hill, Yagoona, and Granville are suburbs illustrative of these processes. In the South Asian community, one can say the tendency to own "McMansions" is evident in the Blacktown area; within the South Asian community, apartment dwellers and those who own McMansions reveal the divide within immigrant ethnic communities. So, space is marked off by all groups large enough to put their stamp on one or several parts of the city, marking off their residential and business areas to develop their communal and economic life.

As discussed earlier, immigrants of lower socio-economic status and many recent entrants are concentrated in medium and high-density apartments closer to commercial centres in the inner and middle rings of the city. Of course, this pattern is, to some extent, determined by the nature of the housing stock available in an area, and the local job market, and amenities. There are several more recent theoretical developments building upon or modifying the two broad perspectives on immigrant assimilation. Segregation research is also largely a quantitative enterprise reliant on indices that measure segregation along a few different dimensions, and geographic scales, testing theories on why ethnic groups tend to cluster together in big cities, and what makes them move away from or settle within resident co-ethnic neighbourhoods and suburbs. Some issues this research grapples with are the nature and extent of segregation, and its causes and effects; additionally, researchers ask if residential clustering translates to segregation in other areas of social life, like work, leisure, or recreation.

Segregation research is also preoccupied with the question of the extent to which residential segregation is related to income and/or occupational distribution. In other words, do immigrants, and non-Whites in particular, face occupational segregation in the formal job market? And does this explain income disparities in the city? If non-White immigrants face occupational and residential segregation, is this a consequence of lack of education and skills, and/or cultural dissimilarity? Does discrimination play a role in the disparities we see in the city? If so, what is the role of discrimination? How can its prevalence and connection to group disparities be explained? These concerns of social science research make it clear that race-neutral discourses of society work towards silencing discussions on race, and through these silences promote a misrecognition of the social problems that dominate everyday life.

We are now at a point where we can summarise our arguments so far to make clearer the connections, complex though they may be, between racism and the disparities in social life. We started off reviewing the debates on housing affordability in Australia and demonstrated how this problem is framed in a race-neutral manner, although race itself is far from being a neutral matter in residential settlement choices or in the organisation of socio-economic activities in urban space. Briefly, house price inflation has outstripped wage growth, making it impossible for people on an average wage to buy a home in Australia's urban centres; this inflation of house prices is also an outcome of political and economic developments that privilege housing over other forms of economic activity, and this in turn has led to the privileging of wealth over income. The literature stresses the institutional factors that led to this predicament, and points to the importance of inheritance as the sole or privileged path towards home ownership. The debates on the asset economy also highlight the inadequacy of income in relation to wealth accumulation. Contrary to these standard arguments, we showed how these official discourses distort our understandings of the correspondence of income and wealth in Australia, and how the matter of White privilege in relation to wealth, inheritance, income, and the material and symbolic value of social space, is hidden or suppressed through race neutral discussions of housing. Our discussion of urban settlement patterns and migrant labour market trends and assimilation uncovers the contested nature of urban space — these are far from being the result of race neutral neo-liberal restructuring. On the contrary, race — specifically White privilege and hegemony in the knowledge economy, bureaucracy, institutionalised politics, and the labour market — plays an instrumental role through its hold over capital and the institutions of government, bureaucracy, and planning to maintain and reproduce White spaces. We could argue that these institutions are indispensable for the continuity and reproduction of White Australia in a time of rising racial diversity. Although the reasons for immigrant clusters are complex, we pointed to the literature on the geography of the private rental market and the proliferation of non-White immigrant clustering in Sydney. We showed the patterns of socio-economic disadvantage, and how these are concentrated in non-White settlement areas. And we hinted at the social distances between these settlements (high density apartments, for example) and the more established and desirable urban spaces synonymous with White Australia.

If all this is valid, we could venture the question: what is a White space in a diverse society? How does it come about? And what does it enable?

Put simply, a White space is a space that enables White social life through primarily being a space where White people are in a majority. This naturally raises the question as to who or what is a White person? Is White a category determined by race, ethnicity, or biology, or are there social and cultural factors that go into the production of the category White? The simplest and easiest answer, well-known in the social sciences today, is that White is a category subject to all manner of changes and adaptations, which include phenotype, and the social and cultural traits that go with a phenotype. Whatever the conditions that give rise to whiteness as a phenotype in society, it is evident that it can only be maintained through social and political institutions that work along the lines of a racial hierarchy and social divide. It is this divide, and the hierarchy of races that this divide is based upon, that manifests in the segmented job market, professions, arts and culture, and the residential settlement patterns of urban Australia. Put differently, White spaces are social spaces that are indispensable for the continuation of White hegemony in Australian society.

Since racial diversity is an established fact in urban Australia, White spaces are not racially homogenous. Yet it is impossible to find a space, be it for work or residence or recreation, occupied predominantly by "White" people, which is not coded by the racialised customs and conventions of whiteness as a way of life, set in opposition to or differentiated from the non-White races. It could be argued that cultural differences necessitate urban spaces to be marked off by all the major ethnicities in urban Australia, and this necessity for communal life applies to the "White" races too. The problem with this kind of thinking about the urban residential mosaic is its innocence about or indifference to the politics of cultural difference, and how such difference is used to sanitise cultural hegemony and its value in the labour market and economy. If "White" people did not consciously and collectively seek to differentiate themselves through the occupational structure, and their residential and cultural preferences, the value of whiteness in society could be subject to the corrosive forces of pluralism and democracy. Further, the symbolic image of Australia as a White society could not be maintained if whiteness did not politically and socially seek to differentiate itself through the institutions of parliamentary democracy, the labour market, the arts and culture, and the public stage. Surely, the institutions of democracy work to bring together the races even as they promote and maintain division along the lines of race in society? The divisions in society are also bound to reflect in and shape the institutions of government and administration. However, amidst this contradictory social scenario, we could say, for our purposes, a White space is a space that enables White ways of acting, thinking, and conceptualising the social world. Such ways of thinking and acting are in conformity with the ideas and myths about a White nation and society. And these ways of thinking and acting are usually traced back to the folk cultures of England, Scotland etc. Yet the emergence of White culture cannot be thought of as separate from the consciousness of a non-White world, outside "Europe" and in "Australia". It is this necessity for a White space to be coded with the customs of whiteness, a category that has historically emerged in opposition to the non-White, and which excludes the non-White other in a hierarchical manner, that requires it to distance itself from the non-White through work and through housing, leisure, and recreation. Surely, the presence of diversity at work, recreation, leisure, and the proliferation of shared public spaces in urban Australia make such an argument seem flawed and problematic. Yet, a close examination of the racial make-up and trends of diversity, be it in consumer tastes, sport, friendship, work, or residential areas, would show that whiteness still maintains its exclusivity and hegemony over the material and symbolic worlds of Australia. Further, the very nature of work, as an example, in organised settings like an office or factory, is far from being free of the compulsions of racial hegemony, as seen not just in the structures and personnel in work spaces, but also in the tacit and not-so-tacit beliefs on the ends of work and its relation to ideas of social welfare, where the social is never free from preconceptions of racial exclusivity predicated on privilege and power. We are arguing, then, for a micropolitics of racial hegemony and how it structures everyday interactions through whiteness. This micropolitics, as seen in organisational structures, is the outcome of larger compulsions of racial dominance. Behind this macro structure of a White racialised labour market and its micro workings, we must see the needs for the reproduction of White hegemony amidst rising diversity and a changing society. On the one hand, we have relentless change coming from immigration, technological change, and globalisation; on the other hand we have the dominance of White privilege, and its hijacking of social processes towards its own necessities, for instance an ageing population importing labour in the name of opportunities in the knowledge economy but then subjecting this labour towards the needs of a racial aristocracy and its affluent lifestyle, coming from wealth and high incomes in the knowledge economy, and through this reproducing the traditional racial hierarchy of Australia.

It is this necessity for the reproduction of the idea of a White Australia that determines the racialised logic of the labour market, and housing in Australia. It is this necessity for whiteness to be synonymous with the official image of a lucky, free, and prosperous nation that determines the distribution of races in the occupational structure, and the ties this occupational structure has with the good Australian homes and the ways of living enabled by such spaces. Again, it is this same politics of whiteness that produces marginality in and through the racial other, through a politics of phenotype that reveals itself in the workings of the labour market and housing wealth. As we said at the outset, it is a mistake to see whiteness as occurring in "nature" and not as produced and reproduced through a relentless logic of socio-political engineering.

In conclusion: when we think of the debates around the labour market in relation to immigration, and the widespread occurrence of what is called discrimination, we cannot afford to view the occurrence or prevalence of racism as isolated or aberrant behaviour. The collective nature of racism in the labour market is a manifestation of the social compulsion behind maintaining the image of a White Australia, and the necessity of maintaining the belief that whiteness is synonymous with professional ability or eligibility, and the non-White is deficient for reasons that include lesser standards in training, education, or cultural suitability. We must not dismiss the view that whiteness itself is an indispensable marker for eligibility and ability in the labour market. In other words, the value of phenotype reigns supreme in the labour market, and this phenomenon itself is an outcome of larger political necessities behind maintaining White supremacy in Australian social life. It is for this reason that White culture cannot be seen as unrelated to efficiency in the job market or creativity in the arts. This is to say that the politics of whiteness, through cultural beliefs and folk practices, promote the myth of whiteness as professionalism, efficiency, and knowledge. In other words, White culture and social life could not be maintained and reproduced without the stranglehold it has on what are seen as and maintained — through the formal economy and labour market — as opportunities for wealth, income, and status in Australia.

Similarly, whatever the economic or social logic/s behind, for example, Nimbyism may be, it is impossible to ignore the necessities of race in the politics around the maintenance of the symbolic and material prestige of White spaces. These spaces, the good homes of Australia and the suburbs they are in, are primarily White spaces, and their location in relation to the labour market as well as the value these locations have, both economically and culturally, cannot be viewed as race neutral. So, we have a situation where race, and phenotype determine the distribution of opportunities in the form of wealth and income in Australia, and socio-economic activity in all forms, including art or medicine or science, is overdetermined by the need for the reproduction of the supremacy of phenotype in Australia.

Works referred to

1. Zubrinsky Charles, Camille *The Dynamics of Racial Residential Segregation* Annual Review of Sociology (2003)